Anonymous

Oregon

It's advantages as an agricultural and commercial state. Statistics, climate,

condition of the people, markets, price of land, wages, cost and routes of

travel

Anonymous

Oregon

It's advantages as an agricultural and commercial state. Statistics, climate, condition of the people, markets, price of land, wages, cost and routes of travel

ISBN/EAN: 9783337148447

Printed in Europe, USA, Canada, Australia, Japan

Cover: Foto ©Andreas Hilbeck / pixelio.de

More available books at **www.hansebooks.com**

OREGON,

ITS

ADVANTAGES AS AN AGRICULTURAL

AND

COMMERCIAL STATE.

———

STATISTICS, CLIMATE, CONDITION OF THE PEO-
PLE, MARKETS, PRICE OF LAND, WAGES,
COST AND ROUTES OF TRAVEL,
ETC., ETC., ETC.

———

Issued by the Board of Statistics, Immigration and Labor
Exchange of
PORTLAND, OREGON,
FOR GRATUITOUS DISTRIBUTION.

PORTLAND, OREGON:
A. G. WALLING, BOOK AND JOB PRINTER.
1870.

INTRODUCTION.

THE BOARD OF STATISTICS, IMMIGRATION AND LABOR EXCHANGE of Portland, Oregon, was organized in August 1869, for the purpose of encouraging immigration into Oregon and to aid immigrants on their arrival, in procuring lands for settlement, or employment for those who need it. Its method of operating is to collect reliable information from all parts of the State, pertaining to the Agricultural and other resources of the country, its climate, soil commercial advantages, markets, price of land, etc., and to disseminate it abroad; to procure information of land for sale or rent and government land for settlement, and to act as a medium between persons who want to employ help of any kind, and those who want employment.

The Association makes no charges for any business it transacts. Funds for its support are obtained by private subscription.

The Association has made its existence known in the States East of the Rocky Mountains, by the distribution of statistical information, through various channels, bearing on the industrial and commercial interests of Oregon. The result of this has been to call forth a great variety of inquiries for more detailed information, coming from all classes of people who, dissatisfied with the harsh climate, and crowded condition of the population in those States, contemplate emigration to the Pacific slope as a measure of relief. That Oregon has attracted general attention from that class of people, is manifest from the great number of these inquiries addressed, not only to this Association, but to Postmasters, Real Estate Agents, Editors of Public Journals and Public Officials throughout the State, evincing a *want* of information regarding the climate and resources of the country.

This pamphlet has been prepared to meet that want. It is intended to be entirely reliable, It embodies facts and statistics drawn from authentic records, from the experience and observations of practical men, and in the absence of these, from the best sources of information attainable. The statements contained in it are as near the actual facts as it is possible to get considering the wide area, the diversity of interests and the sparseness of population.

Oregon wants immigration. All classes of people who pursue industrial avocations are wanted; but more particularly, people acquainted with agricultural pursuits, to occupy and cul-

4

tivate the wide extent of cultivable land now lying idle for the want of population.

The present population of Oregon embraces people of all nationalities, the American predominating largely. As a community they are hospitable, enterprising and progressive. All religious creeds and political opinions are protected alike, both by the laws and public opinion. A family from New England, the Middle, Western or Southern States, arriving in Oregon would find themselves among their countrymen, whose every day avocations are pursued with the same security that they would be in any of the oldest States. People from any nation in Europe coming here, will find representatives from their own country, enjoying all the rights and privileges of American citizens, and pursuing all branches of business.

Society is firmly established. Churches and Schools are numerous, and open to all classes. Life and property have the amplest protection. The condition of the generality of the laboring classes of people is better than in any State in the Union. Wild speculations, financial crises, or mercantile failures have never occurred to an extent sufficient to disarrange the ordinary business affairs of the country. The wealth of Oregon has been accumulated here—drawn from the natural resources of the country.

No great influx of population or capital has ever taken place to build up in a few years a large community, as was the case with some of the North-western States ; on the contrary, everything has grown slowly, but none the less surely.

Remote from the center of population, its great resources and splendid climate are not generally known abroad. To supply this deficiency, at least in part, is the object of this publication. It would be impossible in the small space devoted to the subject to go into very lengthy details, or to embrace the minutia of all branches of business. But those who may desire further information on any subject connected in any way with Oregon interests, whether mentioned here or not, can address the SECRETARY of the BOARD of IMMIGRATION and LABOR EXCHANGE, PORTLAND, OREGON, at whose hands their communications will receive prompt attention.

JOHN M. DRAKE,
Sec'ty Brd. Stat., Im. and Labor Ex.

Portland, Oregon, April, 1870.

GENERAL DESCRIPTION.

Oregon lies between the 42nd and 46th parallels of north latitude, and between the 117th meridian west from Greenwich, and the Pacific Ocean. The State has an average length, east and west, of about 350 miles, and a breadth, north and south, of 275 miles, and contains 96,250 square miles, or, 61,600,000 acres of land. It embraces more territory than the States of New York and Pennsylvania combined. In population it has not to exceed 120,000 inhabitants, while the two States just named contained, according to the census of 1860, an aggregate population of nearly 7,000,000. Of the entire area of the State, about 25,000,000 acres are adapted to agriculture, and about the same quantity to grazing purposes—the remainder being mountain land, valuable only for its immense forests of timber. Of the agricultural and grazing lands, not over six per cent. has passed from the government into the hands of private parties, and the quantity under cultivation would not exceed two per cent.

The Cascade range of mountains, crossing the State from north to south, divides it into two main divisions—the Eastern and Western—each division having its own distinct peculiarities of climate, soil and topography. In the Western Division, lying at the base of, and in in a general parallel direction with, the Cascade range, are three large fertile valleys, separated from each other and from the sea-coast by low ranges of mountains. Taken together, these valleys form a continuous chain of settlements from Northern California to the Columbia river—the orthern boundary of Oregon. The Willamette Valley, the largest of the three, occupies the northern part of the Western Division, with its waters flowing into the Columbia, and navigable the entire length of the valley. The Rogue River Valley lies in the southern part, and the Umpqua Valley between the two. The waters of Rogue River and the Umpqua break through the Coast Range, discharging into the ocean. Rogue River is not navigable, but the Umpqua is navigable for light draft vessels to Scottsburg, twenty-five miles from its mouth; recent attempts to navigate it some forty miles farther up have met with fair success. The valley of the Willamette contains the oldest settlements in Oregon. It is one hundred and twenty-five miles long, and has a breadth of about 40 miles; and in view of all its advantages of soil, climate and marketing facilities, is justly considered to be the finest and best agricultural region of the Pacific slope. The area of its arable lands is sufficient for the support of a million people. Its present population does not exceed eighty thousand. The river flowing through its center drains a large part of the mountain system of Oregon, and with its innumerable tributaries and rivulets furnishes the valley with a constant supply of the best mountain water for agricultural purposes, and with water power for the use of mills and factories. The Umpqua and Rogue River valleys are equally well watered, but are much smaller and of more irregular and uneven surface.

Western Oregon throughout its mountain ranges, and along the coast, is heavily timbered, while the valleys consist of alternate stretches of timber and prairie. Cedar, pine, fir, hemlock, spruce, oak, ash, alder, soft maple and balm, or cottonwood, are the principal varieties of timber adapted to the farmer's use.

Eastern Oregon is an elevated plateau, intersected with numerous water courses flowing in a general northerly direction into the Columbia. The Klamath Basin, situated in the southwestern corner of this division, discharges its waters through the rivers of Northern California. An elevated range, called the Blue Mountains, crosses Eastern Oregon diagonally, from northeast to southwest, spreading out its spurs in all directions across the central and southern parts of that division. This division of the State has a number of fine valleys, including the Grande Ronde, Powder River, Umatilla and John Day valleys in the northern part, the Harney Lake Valley in the central part, and Link River, Lost River, Sprague River and other valleys of the Klamath Basin. It has no navigable rivers except the Columbia on its northern border. The valleys and table lands of this division, comprising more than two-thirds of its entire area, are prairie lands. Timber of excellent quality, embracing several varieties of pine, fir, larch and cottonwood, grows on the high ridges of the mountain ranges and along the water-courses. As a general thing it is convenient of access from the valleys, supplying the settlers with abundant materials for fencing and building purposes. No hard wood is to be found anywhere in the forests of Eastern Oregon, except, at two or three spots along the foot-hills of the Cascade Mountains a scattering growth of oak of an inferior quality for mechanical purposes. The settlements in Eastern Oregon are confined to the valleys of the northern part, and to the mining regions; even there they are quite sparse.

This part of the State has an extensive mining territory, very much of it still undeveloped, and capable of affording employment for labor and capital, for many years, at remunerative rates. The mining population makes a home market for the products of the farms and dairys of the adjacent valleys; an imimportant fact not to be overlooked in forming an estimate of its agricultural advantages.

SOIL AND PRODUCTS.

The valleys of Western Oregon have an undulating surface; so much so, in some places, as to become hilly, while in others, there are broad tracts of land comparatively level. This unevenness of surface occasions frequent alternations of upland and meadow, of timber and prairie; so that the majority of farms have a portion of each. Springs and running brooks supply the farmers with pure water for all household, dairy and stock purposes. In the upper part of the Willamette Valley is an extensive district of smooth prairie land intersected with water courses and groves of timber; and further down the valley are a number of smaller prairies, skirted with heavy bodies of timber. The same conditions exist in the Umpqua and Rogue river valleys, but with the difference that the prairies are smaller in size. The prairie lands just described, together with the gentle slopes of the valleys, are the principal grain lands of Western Oregon. They have a rich soil of dark, sandy loam, very productive, and, generally speaking, easy to cultivate. The products of this kind of land are: wheat, oats, corn, barley, rye, buckwheat, flax, timothy, clover, potatoes, fruit trees, and garden vegetables. Frequent depressions or swales occur, of a stiff black soil, adapted to grass, making excellent meadows when cultivated and seeded to timothy. The hilly portions of the valleys have a soil of dark clay loam, with intervening valleys of sandy loam and vegetable mold, making good grass land, well adapted to grazing purposes and superior for fruit growing. Some of the hilly sections produce a better quality of wheat than even the finest prairie lands, although the yield is not quite so large.

In the northern part of the Willamette valley is an extensive district of country, heavily timbered, on the uplands with fir, hemlock and cedar, and on the swales and creek bottoms with ash, alder, vine maple, and various descriptions of undergrowth. These are among the best lands of the State for grain, grass, fruit trees, and especially for all kinds of root crops and garden vegetables. The mountain lands of the Coast Range are heavily timbered as a general thing. They have a mellow, loamy soil extending in most places to the summits of the ridges. On the western slope of this range, along and near the coast in several places, there are quite extensive districts of high, rolling hills, destitute of timber, and supporting a heavy growth of grass; while the intervening creek bottoms have a rich black soil of great depth. Tide and marsh lands are of frequent occurrence on the coast, producing a fine quality of grass. On Coos Bay, and in that vicinity, are extensive bodies of this kind of land. The grass lands along the coast cannot be excelled in any country for general stock raising purposes ; while the creek bottoms and benches, hardly have an equal for productiveness in all kinds of farm crops.

Wheat and oats are the leading grain crops of Western Oregon. Climate and soil seem to have a special adaptation to their growth, and to the maturity and perfection of the grain. Corn and barley are cultivated to some extent, and good crops of both have been raised in the valleys; but with exceptions in favor of a few localities, they are not regarded as being adapted to the climate. In Rogue river valley, however, barley makes a good crop, yielding from 30 to 50 bushels per acre ; and corn is grown every year in some parts of the Willamette and Umpqua valleys. In the Willamette valley, rye and buckwheat are raised to a small extent, equal probably to the demands of the market. The yield per acre is from 25 to 30 bushels for rye, and 40 to 50 for buckwheat. The buckwheat flour of the Willamette valley is superior to that of any other section on the Pacific slope.

Wheat is a sure crop anywhere in western Oregon. It is free from the ravages of insects, rust, blight, and other deleterious influences common in some sections of the United States. Several varieties of both winter and spring wheat are cultivated; both do well. Winter wheat is put in the ground in October or November, and spring wheat from February to May, according to season, condition of ground, etc. The yield per acre ranges from 20 to 40 bushels ordinarily. Many good farmers claim that with reasonably good cultivation an average of 30 bushels one year with another can be depended on. In the history of the white settlement of Western Oregon, extending over a period of about 30 years, there has never been a failure of the wheat crop; and only twice during that time was there sufficient rain in harvest time to damage the crop. The quality of the grain is superior. It attains to more than the ordinary weight per bushel, and makes a quality of flour that commands the highest prices in San Francisco and New York. Frequently the San Francisco market reports quote the flour of some of the principal mills of Oregon at figures above anything of California manufacture. A cargo of wheat shipped in the spring of 1869, by a business firm of Portland, to Liverpool, entered into competition with wheat from all parts of the world, and brought the highest price current at the time.

Oats is the principal grain raised for feed, particularly in the Umpqua and Willamette valleys. It is always a sure crop, and yields all the way from 50 to 100 bushels per acre. A large quantity is shipped every year to San Francisco, where it sells from 10 to 15 cents per hundred pounds higher than that produced in California.

As an example of the productiveness of Western Oregon of the two leading grain crops, an extract is here given from an address delivered by Hon. A. J. Dufur, late President of the Oregon State Agricultural Society, before the American Institute Farmers' Club in New York City, September 25th, 1869 :

Allow me to cite some well authenticated facts to prove the fertility of our Oregon lands. In Linn county, as President of the Agricultural Society of the State, I had the pleasure of awarding the premium to a farmer who raised 82 bushels of oats to the acre, weighing 43 pounds per bushel ; for the best 10 acres in oats, a premium for 78 bushels per acre, weight 41 pounds per bushel ; for the best 10 acres of wheat, showing 48 bushels per acre. And to another farmer a premium for a field of oats, measuring 85 bushels to the acre. In Marion county the average yield of wheat is 33½ bushels per acre. I have known 3,500 bushels grown on 69½ acres, and the grain weighed 66 pounds per bushel.

And again, from the Oregon *Statesman*, Oct. 21st, 1869 :

There are on Howell prairie, (in Marion county) six men living close together, who this year harvested an aggregate of 315 acres of wheat, yielding 10,846 bushels, or nearly 34½ bushels per acre. This has been a poor wheat season, and Howell prairie is no better than the rest of Marion county. One of the same men, A. B. Simmons, selected six acres from his forty of oats, and measured up from the six acres, six hundred bushels.

In the Willamette Valley the cultivation of flax is beginning to engage the attention of farmers to a considerable extent. The seed used is the Bombay variety, yielding a large crop of seed, but producing a fibre of inferior quality and small in quantity. The upland ridges have been found best adapted to it. The yield ranges from 25 to 30 bushels per acre. The California Oil Mills have contracted, this year, for the product of 6,000 acres in Linn county, the seed to be delivered at Albany at 2½ cents per pound ; and the Pioneer Oil Mills, at Salem, in this State, have contracted for the product of 3,000 acres, at the same figures, delivered at their mills.

Fruit of nearly every description is raised with unusual success. The trees come into full bearing in three years from transplanting, and with very little care or cultivation yield heavy crops of fruit of the finest quality. Apples, pears, plums, quinces, cherries, currants and all descriptions of small fruits and berries have a special adaptation to the moist climate and sea air of Western Oregon. Peaches, apricots, grapes and that class of fruits loving a hot, dry climate, do not succeed so well in the northern part of the Willamette Valley and along the coast; but in Rogue River Valley and the hilly country west of it, where the climate is hotter and dryer, more nearly approaching that of California, that class of fruit is cultivated very successfully. Thus far fruit trees in Oregon have been entirely exempt from the diseases incident to their cultivation in the majority of the older States.

Among the grasses, timothy, blue grass and clover, are the kinds mostly cultivated—the former to a large extent as a hay crop. On the swales and ash bottoms it yields from two to three tons per acre, very often without any cultivation except to sow the seed after the ground has been cleared of its growth of brush and burnt over. The abundant growth of wild grass renders unnecessary any extensive cultivation of grass for pasturing purposes.

Garden vegetables of all kinds, and the various root crops, are cultivated very successfully in all parts, particularly so on the timber lands and creek bottoms, where the yield of these products is very large. Except in a few instances for gardening purposes, irrigation of the soil is not practiced in Western Oregon. The abundant rains of spring and early summer, together with the fertility of the soil, renders it entirely unnecessary.

Eastern Oregon consists of high table lands and rolling prairies, with a number of valleys along its water courses, of considerable extent. Taken as a whole, it is especially adapted to grazing purposes, although its valleys contain farming lands equal in productiveness to those of any country; and in many places the high prairies have produced excellent crops of grain. North of the Blue Mountains, or what is known as the Great Plain of the Columbia, the soil of the highlands is a sandy loam, producing in its natural state a heavy growth of wild bunch grass of the most nutritious quality. In the central and southern portions of this division of the State, the highlands are rugged and broken, the surface of the country, sometimes for miles in extent, being covered with broken trap rock; still, with the exception of a few barren spots, the growth of bunch grass is undiminished either in quantity or quality. It springs up fresh and green, in the first warm days of early spring, and in a few weeks stock begins to fatten on it. By burning over the ground, a fall growth is produced, which, by the middle of October, makes good grazing and lasts through the short winter of that section of the country. It was the custom of the Indians of Eastern Oregon, in former years, to raise large herds of horses without providing any feed for them for the winter. The settlers and stock-raisers there now raise and fatten, every year, thousands of cattle, grazing them the year round. Fat beef cattle, wintered and fattened on the "range," have been shipped down the Columbia, and thence to Victoria, on Vancouver's Island, to market, as early in the spring as the middle of March.

The valleys of Eastern Oregon have a rich soil of black loam, producing wheat, oats, barley, corn, vegetables and fruits. Wheat succeeds equally as well as in Western Oregon, while barley does much better, often yielding as high as 60 to 80 bushels per acre. Corn makes a good crop in many of the valleys, the warm, dry summer weather of this region being adapted to its growth and maturity. Some of the tender fruits and vegetables, as peaches, grapes, melons, tomatoes and sweet potatoes, are being cultivated with good success. Tobacco has succeeded well in several instances. In a general sense, the range of farm products varies very little from that of Western Oregon, making due allowance for the different adaptabilities of a dry climate. Irrigation is resorted to occasionally for the better production of garden vegetables and fruits; but thus far, it has not been found necessary in the cultivation of any kind of grain crops. This part of Oregon has been settled but a few years, and experience has not demonstrated conclusively whether there is any liability of the failure of crops from drought or other causes; although the success attending farm operations thus far, would indicate that no dangers of that nature are to be apprehended. It is claimed by the people of Eastern Oregon, that for productiveness its valleys cannot be excelled on the Pacific Slope. The absence of timber in the valleys is considered a disadvantage by some; this, however, is more apparent than otherwise, from the fact that the neighboring mountains afford an inexhaustible supply. Water of good quality is plenty in all the valleys, but the number of springs and running brooks is much less than in Western Oregon.

CLIMATE.

To give an account of the climate of any one county in the State of Ohio would be to describe the climate of the entire State, in the main. Not so with Oregon, where the extent of territory is so great, that the various influences of mountain ranges, extended plains, contiguity to the sea, the prevailing winds and other causes operate to make a climate as varied as are the peculiarities of its numerous localities. Latitude on the North-west coast of America is no index to the character of the climate. Astoria, at the mouth of the Columbia River, situated on the same degree of latitude, nearly, with Quebec, has a summer temperature 8° cooler, and a winter temperature 30° warmer than that place. It is only in the high altitudes of the mountain ranges, that deep snows and harsh winters have any existence in Oregon.

The following table, compiled chiefly from the reports of the Smithsonian Institute, will give a comparative view of the temperature of the four seasons, at several prominent points on the North Pacific slope, with that of a number of places East of the Rocky Mountains. The only point in Eastern Oregon embraced in the table is the Dalles, at the Eastern base of the Cascade range; a place influenced to a great extent by local causes, and does not fairly represent the climate in the extensive valleys farther East, constituting the principal agricultural and grazing districts of Eastern Oregon.

Table.—Showing comparative mean Temperature.

	Latitude	Spring.	Summer	Fall.	Winter.	Average.
Astoria, Oregon	46.10	51.16	61.36	53.55	42.43	52.13
Corvallis, "	44.30	52.19	67.13	53.41	39.27	53.00
The Dalles "	45.40	53.00	70.36	52.21	35.59	52.79
Steilacoom, W. T.	47.10	49.00	62.00	51.00	39.00	50.00
Augusta, Ill.	40.10	51.34	72.51	53.38	29.80	51.76
Hazlewood, Minn	44.20	42.33	69.95	42.60	13.06	41.97
Albany, N. Y.	42.35	47.61	70.17	50.01	25.83	48.41
Quebec, C. E.	46.50	40.00	69.00	45.00	12.00	41.00
New York City	40.45	48.00	72.00	54.00	31.00	51.00
Norfolk, Va.	36.50	56.00	76.00	61.00	40.00	59.00

It will be seen from the above that Corvallis, situated in latitude 44.30, and in the heart of the Willamette valley, has a winter temperature nearly the same as Norfolk, situated nearly eight degrees further South, while the summer temperature of the latter place is nearly nine degrees higher than that of the former. It is this comparative evenness of temperature throughout the year that gives to the climate of Oregon its greatest charm.

The first thing that impresses a stranger in passing from Western into Eastern Oregon is the very decided change noticeable everywhere, in the atmosphere, vegetation and general aspect of the country. This is due chiefly to the difference in the climate of the two sections: Western Oregon has a wet climate, while the Eastern part has a dry one.

The winter of Eastern Oregon, though of short duration, generally brings with it several inches of snow on the table lands and in the valleys. The weather is usually dry but quite cold. Snow remains from three to six weeks, in the months of December and January, some seasons; in others, only a few days. It is usual for stock to be grazed through these months without interruption, but occasionally there is a "hard winter," rendering it necessary to do some feeding. The Spring begins in February and lasts to the end of May, with warm pleasant weather, and rain sufficient to give life and vigor to vegetation. The summers are hot and dry, but not sultry or oppressive. It is very seldom that rain falls in summer or early fall, still the freshness of the mountain air renders the days pleasant and the nights cool and refreshing. The range of the thermometer is rather above the summer temperature of Western Oregon; sometimes reaching 100°, but only at rare intervals. Ordinarily, the thermometer indicates 90° as about the highest summer temperature, and 10° as the lowest for winter, although these limits may not mark the extremes in the case of an uncommonly hard winter, or warm summer, occurring once in from five to eight years.

The amount of rain fall in Western Oregon is regarded by some as an objection to the climate. The rain fall, though large, has been generally over rated. The following table prepared by Thomas Frazar, Esq., of Portland, from notes carefully kept during a course of ten years, will furnish the facts:

WEATHER RECORD FOR OREGON.

From the *Daily Oregonian* of Nov. 18th, 1869 :—As the impression is abroad in many of the States, as also in Oregon, that Oregon has a greater number of *stormy* or rainy days than any other State, I send you the enclosed table of the weather, which I have kept *daily* for the past ten years, beginning April, 1858 ; which table will show that Oregon has a yearly average of 65 per cent. of days without *rain* or *snow*. Besides this a large proportion of the days recorded under the head of "sunshine and showers," were days in which persons could follow their out-door vocations without serious inconvenience. Under the head of "pleasant" no rain or snow fell between sunrise and sunset. Under the head of "rainy," there was no sunshine, and rain fell most of the time. Under the head of "sunshine and showers," are included days when a part or half of the day would be pleasant and part rainy. I am aware that rain and snow fell during the time between sunset and sunrise, also that many days that are marked rainy, the night would be clear and pleasant. I think one will offset the other. I have also noted some of the *extremes* during some years, which you can publish if you think them deserving of notice. I think the table will be appreciated by persons interested in or inquiring about Oregon :

1858.

MONTHS	Pleasant	Rainy	Sunshine & shower	Snowed	MONTHS	Pleasant	Rainy	Sunshine & shower	Snowed
April..20	6	4	...		Sep....21	5	4	...	
May ..15	6	10	...		Oct ...18	6	7	...	
June..23	3	4	...		Nov....18	8	3	...	
July...27	1	1	...		Dec ...10	11	6	4	
Aug...25	2	4	...		Total180	48	43	4	
1859.					**1859.**				
Jan ...18	9	4	...		July...29	...	2	...	
Feb ... 4	10	6	8		Aug ...25	3	3	...	
March 4	12	9	6		Sep....20	8	2	...	
April...21	3	6	...		Oct.....22	6	3	...	
May...20	8	3	...		Nov ...18	8	3	1	
June..	25	5	...		Dec....22	6	1	2	
Total ...228					Total ...228	73	47	17	
1860.					**1860.**				
Jan ...19	10	1	1		July...27	1	3	...	
Feb ...16	9	3	1		Aug ...24	3	4	...	
Mar...18	6	6	1		Sep....23	5	2	...	
April..14	4	11	...		Oct ...17	10	4	...	
May...15	8	8	...		Nov ...18	8	4	...	
June...25	2	3	...		Dec ...16	8	1	...	
Total ...232					Total ...232	72	57	5	
1861.					**1861.**				
Jan ...16	6	6	3		July ..29	...	2	...	
Feb... 14	12	2	...		Aug ...27	1	3	...	
Mar ...19	2	9	1		Sep....26	2	2	...	
April..16	5	9	...		Oct....19	6	6	...	
May ..18	5	8	...		Nov... 8	16	4	2	
June...17	6	7	...		Dec....15	9	3	4	
Total ...224					Total ...224	70	61	10	
1862.					**1862.**				
Jan ...20	2	1	8		July...28	1	7	...	
Feb...17	4	3	4		Aug ...28	2	1	..	
Mar ...13	7	9	2		Sep....25	4	1	...	
April. 19	4	5	2		Oct....23	4	4	...	
May ..17	4	10	...		Nov...28	1	1	...	
June ..21	2	7	...		Dec ...16	12	3	...	
Total ... 250					Total ... 250	47	52	16	
1863.					**1863.**				
Jan ...11	17	1	2		July...27	2	2	...	
Feb...10	7	8	3		Aug....29	...	2	...	
Mar...19	6	4	2		Sep....19	4	7	...	
April..15	8	6	1		Oct.....20	8	3	...	
May...22	2	7	...		Nov....14	10	6	...	
June ..27	1	2	...		Dec.... 7	17	7	...	
Total...220					Total...220	82	55	8	

1864.

MONTHS	Pleasant	Rainy	Sunshine & shower	Snowed	MONTHS	Pleasant	Rainy	Sunshine & shower	Snowed
Jan ...15	8	3	5		July ..28	...	3	...	
Feb ...24	4	1	...		Aug ...27	...	4	...	
Mar ...14	8	9	...		Sept ..17	6	7	...	
April .23	5	2	...		Oct.....25	3	3	...	
May...29	...	2	...		Nov ..16	11	3	...	
June.. 19	4	7	...		Dec ...15	11	3	2	
Total ...252	60	47	7						
1865.					**1865.**				
Jan ...17	11	2	1		July ..26	1	4	...	
Feb ...18	6	3	1		Aug ..25	...	6	...	
Mar ...13	10	4	4		Sep....13	7	10	...	
April .20	5	5	...		Oct..23...	...	8	...	
May...25	3	3	...		Nov...14	11	5	...	
June..22	3	5	...		Dec....11	8	8	4	
Total ...227	65	63	10						
1866.					**1866.**				
Jan ...19	7	2	3		July ..30	...	1	...	
Feb....17	3	8	...		Aug ..26	1	4	...	
Mar...15	11	5	...		Sept...29	...	1	...	
April..14	7	9	...		Oct ...17	9	5	...	
May...18	5	8	...		Nov...15	11	4	...	
June..14	6	10	...		Dec....16	13	2	...	
Total ... 230	73	59	3						
1867.					**1867.**				
Jan...16	10	2	3		July ..18	3	10	...	
Feb ..10	12	5	1		Aug...30	...	1	...	
Mar...27	2	1	1		Sep ...26	3	1	...	
April .19	4	7	...		Oct.....20	5	6	..	
May...23	2	6	...		Nov...19	8	3	...	
June .25	3	2	...		Dec....11	13	5	2	
Total ...244	65	49	7						
1868.					**1868.**				
Jan ...23	2	1	5		July...30	1	...	...	
Feb ...21	3	4	1		Aug...31	...	...	...	
Mar...14	3	12	2		Sep....29	1	...	...	
April..18	4	8	...		Oct.....27	1	3	...	
May...19	3	9	...		Nov...20	6	4	...	
June .23	1	6	...		Dec....17	5	8	1	
Total ...272	30	55	9						

Recapitulation.

	Pleasant	Rainy	Sunshine & shower	Snowed		Pleasant	Rainy	Sunshine & shower	Snowed
1858* 180	48	43	4		1864 252	60	47	7	
1859 228	73	47	17		1865 227	65	63	10	
1860 232	72	57	5		1866 230	73	59	3	
1861 224	70	61	10		1867 244	65	49	7	
1862 250	47	52	16		1868 272	30	55	9	
1863 220	82	55	8						
					Total...2559	685	588	96	

*Nine months.

Sixty-five per cent. of the above days are without rain or snow.

NOTES.—Ice formed December 2d, 1858, In 1859 ponds were frozen over at times till March 1st—ice never over two inches thick ; very little cold weather in December, 1859 ; no ice to speak of. January 24th, 1860, the ground froze for the first time this winter—first ice Jan. 26th. Ice and frost all gone Feb. 1st. I planted potatoes Feb. 6th ; on the 17th planted onion sets and onion seeds; April 26th planted corn. Jan. 2d, 1862, Columbia river frozen over so that the ocean steamers could not run ; thermometer 16° below freezing point. Jan. 8th, snow a foot deep ; excellent sleighing. On 17th, Willamette frozen hard enough to cross on foot. On 24th, ice gone out of Willamette river. March 10th, snow all disappeared. January 7th, 1868, Columbia river closed with ice. On the 11th Willamette closed over so as to stop the steamers running to Oregon City until the 28th. No rain fell after the first of July until September 3d—63 days—and then none again till October 23d. THOS. FRAZAR.

These observations were taken at Portland where there is about as much rain as at any place in Oregon. The upper part of the Willamette Valley has considerably less; Umppua Valley still less : and Rogue River less than either, the climate becoming dryer, going South from the Columbia River, so that in the Southern part of the State it approaches that of California.

The following figures show the rain fall in inches, for each season and for the whole year, at New York, St. Louis and San Francisco, as compared with Astoria.

	Spring.	Summer.	Fall.	Winter.	Year.
Astoria.................................	16	4	17	22	59
San Francisco........................	8	0	2	11	21
New York.............. .\	11	11	9	10	41
St. Louis.............................	12	· 14	8	6	40

In a strict sense of the term, Western Oregon has but two seasons—the wet and dry. An ordinary rainy season begins early in November and continues to the first of April, usually, with intermissions of good weather in January and February of a few days or a few weeks duration. These intervals are generally accompanied by a few inches of snow, raw, cold weather, and sharp frosts, constituting the only approach to actual winter to which the country is subject. Stock in all sheltered localities get along through these cold snaps without feed, especially when pasture has been reserved for such emergencies. It is safe to assert that two-thirds of the stock of the valleys go through all ordinary winters by taking care of themselves in the pastures and woods; while along the coast, where tide and marsh lands are accessible, owners of stock do not pretend to feed. Once in seven or eight years, there comes what is called a "hard winter;" that is, the winter interval continues six weeks or two months; snow remains on the ground several weeks; the cold weather is prolonged until the water courses freeze. At such times stock will suffer unless it recieves some attention. To offset the "hard winter," there occurs sometimes a very mild one, like the season of 1868-69, with not even enough snow to whiten the ground, or cold to form ice thicker than a window glass.

Gardening operations were commenced in February that season, and flowers bloomed in the open air throughout the winter. There have been a number of such seasons in Oregon within fifteen or twenty years.

From April to the end of June, the weather is usually warm, pleasant and showery. The dry season proper, commences about the first of July and continues to the end of October, interrupted by a week's rainy weather in September. The term "dry season," as applied to Oregon, does not imply excessive heat and sultriness, for such it not the case. The prevailing wind is from the North-west—a sea breeze that keeps the temperature down. The nights are cool and refreshing to men who do out door work, although the effect is not beneficial so far as corn raising is concerned. The extremes of heat and cold in Western Oregon may be put at 14° for the lowest and 82° as the highest range of the thermometer, although a few instances have occurred in which these limits were passed.

A noticeable feature of Western Oregon, due mainly to the climate, is the excessive luxuriance of all kinds of vegetation, especially on the Columbia and along the coast. The country wears an appearance of perpetual spring. An Oregon fir tree often reaches an altitude of three hundred feet, or over eighteen rods; trees, out of which have been taken eigteen rail-cuts, and many of which will make from six to ten thousand feet of lumber. The common elder becomes in this moist climate, a tree of ten or twelve inches in diameter, and the alder grows large enough for saw-logs.

Another noticeable feature is, that, although a *rainy* country, Oregon is not subject to high tempests, terrific hailstorms, earthquakes or other like phenomena, so common and so destructive in some States. Observations made by government officers show that in twenty-one years Oregon had only three winds moving at the rate of forty-five miles an hour, with a force of ten pounds to the square foot. In Massachusetts, Rhode Island and Connecticut, the reports from eleven stations where observations were made, show that in thirty months there were four winds of forty-five miles velocity and ten pounds power, and two winds of sixty miles velocity and eighteen pounds power. At eleven stations in Indiana, Illinois, Michigan, Iowa and Wisconsin, the reports show that during twenty-six months there were twenty-five winds of forty-five miles velocity, two winds of seventy-five miles velocity, and two hurricanes of a velocity of ninety miles an hour.

From a register of meteorological observations kept at the Portland Library rooms, the following record of the weather is compiled for the months of January and February, 1870:

January : Highest temperature ....63°
Lowest " 17
Highest average for one day 57
Lowest " " 23
Mean temperature for the month 40
Rain fall for the month ....4.83 inches.
Snow " " ....½ inch.
February: Highest temperature ....58°
Lowest " 32
Highest average for one day 49
Lowest " " 36
Average for the month 42½
Total rain fall ....4.30 inches.
Snow ....none.

These observations are useful as indicating the range of the thermometer at a season of the year when sudden changes are most likely to occur.

Observations carefully kept by Dr. I. Moses, U. S. A., at Astoria, for a period of fourteen months, commencing August, 1850, and terminating September 1851, show that, during that period the greatest variation of the thermometer during any one month was 37°. The highest points reached by the mercury during the period was 94°; the lowest, 22°. The highest daily mean, 82°; the lowest, 26°. Variation during the coldest day, 6°; during the warmest day, 12°. Mean annual temperature, 53°. The Doctor remarks that, "These observations may be considered the average of the temperature, year after year, at that place, and when it is considered that Astoria is in about the same latitude as Houlton, Maine, and Sault St. Marie, the uniformity and mildness of the climate seem remarkable."

HEALTHFULNESS OF THE CLIMATE.

The experience of the early missionaries, the employees of the Hudson's Bay Company, and the American settlers that followed them, during the course of a period of thirty years, is that the climate of Oregon is a healthy one. In comparing the rates of mortality in the Pacific States with that of some of the States east of the Rocky Mountains, the following facts are obtained : The deaths in Arkansas in 1860, were at the rate of one person out of every 48 ; Massachusetts and Louisiana lost one in 57 ; Illinois and Indiana, one in 87 ; Kansas, one in 68 ; Vermont, the healthiest State on the Atlantic slope, lost one in 92 ; California lost one in 101 ; Oregon, one in 172, and Washington Territory, one in 228. The difference in favor of the climate of the Pacific coast is really greater than the figures make it ; for a great many persons afflicted with incurable complaints, have gone there in the hope of obtaining some sort of relief.

On this subject an article written by Dr. Wm. H. Watkins, of Portland, a physician of seventeen years practice in different parts of Oregon and Washington Territory, is introduced to illustrate whatever effect the climate may have on particular forms of disease as compared with that of several other States. The Doctor writes :

"Oregon, in truth, may be said to have no prevailing type of disease. In the Willamette Valley we have the soil, the alluvial deposit, the moisture, which, in Indiana or Illinois, would cause agues and intermittents to be rife through the community,—and throughout the valley in spring and autumn occasional cases of ague are found, but they invariably yield to remedies in small doses compared with those given in malarial districts in the Western States. Very rarely is a person seen with the ague cachexia- and complexion, so often seen in the ague districts of the Wabash, Illinois and Sacramento Valleys. The type is commonly a tertian, or when a chill occurs every other day, though persons having a chill daily are met with.

For this somewhat remarkable immunity from malarial disorders, considering the extent and depth of our river bottoms, we are indebted to our northern latitude, to the daily sea-breeze borne to us from the waters of the Pacific, to our cool, bracing nights, and to the medium temperature of even our warmest days. Typhus or typhoid fevers have never been epidemic in Oregon.

The equable temperature, summer and winter, the absence of high cold winds and sudden atmospheric changes, render people less subject to bronchial, rheumatic and inflammatory complaints than they are in countries where the thermometer swings entirely around the circle. In July and August, as at the East, children are troubled with summer complaint, but the disease is ordinarily quite amenable to treatment, and seldom runs into dysentery.

East of the Cascades the air is dry, the altitude high, and the country is popularly supposed to be beneficial to consumptives. Army reports appear to sanction this belief.

On the head waters of the Columbia a disease somewhat peculiar, known as mountain fever, attacks the inhabitants, if particularly exposed. It probably is malarial in its origin, but is modified by the rarity and dryness of the atmosphere. It

presents many features of remittent fever, is disposed to take a
typhoid type with congestions of brain, lungs or bowels. It
naturally tends to resolution as but few die. While at Fort
Walla Walla, I attended twenty-two cases, soldiers who had
made a summer and fall campaign up the waters of Snake river,
all of whom recovered.

For twenty years, aside from scarlet fever and dyptheria,
which several years ago visited nearly every neighborhood,
there has been no general epidemic of at all fatal character in
Oregon. The general salubrity of the climate and healthfulness
of the people cannot be questioned.

I append some statistics of mortality taken from the report of
the Surgeon General of the army from several sections of the
country :

DEATHS FROM FEVER.

New England	1 in 283.
Harbor of New York	1 in 66.
The Great Lakes	1 in 159.
Jefferson Barracks and St. Louis Arsenal	1 in 113.
Texas. Southern frontier	1 in 67.
Texas, Western frontier	1 in 529.
Oregon and Washington Territory	1 in 529.

POLITICAL SUBDIVISIONS.

Oregon is divided into twenty-two counties, viz : Baker, Ben-
ton, Clackamas, Clatsop, Columbia, Coos, Curry, Douglass,
Grant, Jackson, Josephine, Linn, Lane, Marion, Multnomah,
Polk. Tillamook, Union, Umatilla, Wasco, Washington and
Yamhill.

BAKER county, is situated east of the Cascade mountains,
and presents a good field for settlement. During the past year
a marked increase has been noticed both in population and wealth
of this county. 'Auburn, the county seat is located about 350
miles from Portland by the usual traveled route. Baker City,
an important trading point; is located about ten miles southeast
of Auburn, in the Powder river valley. Taxable property of the
county, $418,490. This county embraces one of the largest
mining districts in the State.

BENTON county, situated in the heart of the Willamette valley, contains a population of 4,669 with assessable property valued at $1,133,097. Corvallis, the county seat, is one of the hand-
somest towns in the State and is a place of considerable trade.
It contains several excellent schools, a college conducted by
the Methodist Church South, a Female Academy under the

auspices of the Episcopalians. three Churches, Methodist, Presbyterian and Catholic. The Corvallis *Gazette*, a weekly newspaper, is published here. Assessed valuation of property in Corvallis for 1869, $374,347 79.

CLATSOP county contains a population of about 1,200 ; voters 250 ; acres of land under cultivation, 3,000 ; value of assessable property, $325,000. Astoria, the county seat, is pleasantly located on the left bank of the Columbia river, about ten miles above its mouth, and about 100 miles northwest of Portland During the past year many additional buildings have been erected, and when the custom house now in contemplation has been completed, Astoria will present quite a city-like appearance. Astoria derives its name from John Jacob Astor, whose employees founded a fur depot at this point on the 12th of April, 1811.

CLACKAMAS county combines within its limits all the elements that when properly developed tend to make a country prosperous. Immense water power exists along its river bank; the Oswego iron works, with its unlimited supply of ore, skirt it on the north, whilst its agricultural lands are extensive as well as excellent. Oregon City, the county seat, was formerly the seat of the Territorial Legislature, and is the oldest incorporated town in Oregon. All the merchandise and produce passing up and down the Willamette valley goes through Oregon City, and each year witnesses a marked improvement in its prospects. Its present population is about 1,300. A flourishing graded school is in operation, with an attendance of nearly 200 scholars. The population of Clackamas county is estimated at 6,000. Voters, 1,250. Value of assessable property, $1,532,924. Oregon City is the seat of a U. S. Land Office.

COLUMBIA county is situated on the Columbia river, the boundary between Oregon and Washington Territory. This county contains a population of about 500. Number of voters, 220. Acres of land under cultivation, 1,000. Value of assessable property, $167,245. St. Helens, the county seat, is pleasantly located on the bank of the Columbia river, and promises to be a place of much commercial importance. Lumber is extensively manufactured at this point, and during the past year the growth of the town has received quite an impetus. This county contains nearly 300,000 acres of unimproved land, some extensive, but undeveloped, mines of coal and iron, and valuable salt springs.

COOS county, situated in the southwestern part of the State, on the coast, contains a population of about 1,200, with assessable property valued at $432,273. Number of voters, 500. Gold, copper, iron and coal have been found to exist in this county, and the coal mines have already proved a source of great wealth. Lumber is manufactured extensively at North Bend, situate about ten miles from Empire City, the county seat. Ship building is also carried on in this county.

CURRY county, the most southwesterly portion of the State, contains a smaller population than any other county in Oregon. This may be accounted for from the fact that it is remote from the tide of immigration which annually flows into the State. Indications of copper ore have been found within its borders, and gold mines have been discovered and worked at Port Orford, on the coast. Ellensburg, the county seat, is situate on the southern bank of Rogue River. Taxable property of the county, $110,494.

DOUGLAS county contains an area of about 5,000 square miles. About 25,000 acres of land are under cultivation. The population numbers about 9,000. Value of assessable property, $1,474,704. Number of voters, 1,400. No county in the State presents a greater diversity of scenery than does Douglas. Roseburg, the county seat, is a thriving town of about five hundred inhabitants. It is conveniently located on the direct stage route from Portland to Sacramento, and contains Episcopal and Methodist Churches, schools and a court house. A U. S. Land Office is located here.

This county embraces the entire Umpqua Valley, and is one of the best stock counties in the State. It contained in 1869, 11,000 head of cattle, 160,000 sheep, and produced 480,000 lbs. of wool. The county expended the same year $4,294 on roads and bridges, and paid its school teachers $2,474 in currency and $3,044 in coin.

GRANT county, situated in Eastern Oregon, contains a population of about 3,000. Number of voters, 750. This county contains large tracts of excellent grazing lands, and numerous sections of agricultural soil. Gold mines have been discovered within its borders, and good paying diggings are being worked very extensively. Canyon City, the county seat, is a mining town of considerable importance. It is situated on the middle fork of John Day's river, and is distant from Portland about 314 miles. The county has about 3,000 acres of land under cultivation. Taxable property, $321,604. Its estimated yield of gold since the discovery of the mines in 1861, is $10,000,000.

JACKSON county covers an area of about 8,000 square miles, with a population of 6,000. Number of voters, 1,300. This county combines within its limits agricultural, manufacturing and mineral resources which will tend to render it in future of great importance to the balance of the State. For nearly eighteen years the gold mines of this country have been successfully worked, and even now they yield sufficient to repay for the outlay of capital and labor expended in working them. Jacksonville, the county seat, is a prosperous place, containing within its corporate limits many handsome buildings. The Methodists, Catholics and other denominations have churches here, with several public and private schools. The sisters of the Most Holy Names have an academy for young ladies. This county embraces the whole of Rogue River Valley. It has about 15,000 acres of land under cultivation. Taxable property, $1,023,814. A fine woolen mill is in operation at Ashland.

JOSEPHINE county covers an area of 2,500 square miles, with but four thousand acres under cultivation. The principal source of the wealth of this county arises from its gold mines which are annually being developed. Large tracts of good arable land are yet unoccupied in this county, and offer good homes to industrious settlers. Kirbyville, the county seat, is situated on the Illinois river, which flows through the Illinois valley, and is a lively town of growing importance. Taxable property, $212,553. Number of voters, 350.

LINN county—one of the best agricultural districts in Oregon—covers an area of 1,400,000 acres. Population, 8,000. Number of voters, 2,308. Value of assessable property, $2,960,-694. Acres of land under cultivation, about 100,000. Albany, the county seat, is situated on the east bank of the Willamette river, about seventy-five miles south of Portland. It is pleasantly located, and each recurring year adds to its population, wealth and importance. The town comprises several brick stores, a large number of frame buildings, a court house, which cost upwards of $30,000, two flouring mills, four churches, a college, public schools, and all the other accessories of civilization. Two weekly newspapers are published at Albany. Harrisburg and Peoria are each prominent shipping points on the Willamette river in this county.

LANE county covers an area of about 3,500 square miles and embraces within its limits some of the finest agricultural lands in Oregon. About sixty thousand acres of land are under cultivation in this county, and the value of taxable property is assessed at $1,769,780. Eugene City, the county seat, contains a population of about 2,000. It is situated at the head of steamboat navigation on the Willamette river, and contains an indus-, trious and enterprising people. Among the public institutions of Eugene City may be mentioned a commodious court house, an academy and several public and private schools. The Catholics, Presbyterians, Episcopalians, Baptists and Methodists have each a church here. The office of the United States Surveyor General is at this place. The county extends from the summit of the Cascades to the coast, and covers the southern part of the Willamette valley. It has a population of about 8,000. Number of voters, 1,400.

MARION county covers an area of nearly 3,000 square miles. Its central position, excellent soil and commercial advantages renders Marion county one of the most prosperous portions of Oregon. Salem, the capital of the State and the county seat, is delightfully located on the east bank of the Willamette river, presenting a handsomer appearance than any other town in Oregon. This county has a population of 10,500. Voters, 2,500. Value of assessable property, $3,174,919. Salem can boast of more church edifices than any town of its size on the Pacific coast. The religious organizations represented by churches, are the Methodists, whose first building was erected in 1841; Congregationalists, organized in 1853; Baptists, organized in 1859. The Catholic, Episcopalian, Campbellite, Evangelical Association, and Methodist Church South, organized more recently. The Oregon *Statesman*, Willamette *Farmer* and *Democratic Press* are published at Salem.

The Willamette University, the most prominent educational institution in the State, is located here. Salem is the seat of considerable manufacturing enterprise, having a woolen mill, an oil mill, several large flouring and saw mills and an iron foundry in successful operation. The assessed value of town property, for 1869, is $1,394,158. Population, 3,500.

MULTNOMAH county, although the smallest in size, is the wealthiest county in the State. Population, about 11,000. Number of voters, 2,500. Value of taxable property, $5,944,-766. This county is situated in the extreme northern part of the Willamette Valley. It is bounded by the Columbia river on the north, and embraces within its limits the triangle formed by the junction of the Willamette with the Columbia river.

THE CITY OF PORTLAND, situated in latitude 45° 30′ north, and longitude 122° 27′ west, the county seat of Multnomah county, and the commercial capital of Oregon, is also the depot whence the people of a region of country larger than New England and the Middle States combined, derive their supplies, including Eastern Oregon, and a large portion of the Territories of Idaho, Washington and Montana. The city is pleasantly located on the west bank of the Willamette river, twelve miles above its junction with the Columbia, and 110 miles from the sea, by the course of the river. It is located on a plateau which gradually ascends as it recedes from the river until it forms a range of hills at the western extremity of the city, from which may be seen the summits of several mountain peaks in the Cascade range, clothed in perpetual snow.

Commercially speaking, Portland is the key to the entire Willamette and Columbia river valleys, being the *entrepot* at which arrives all the merchandise, goods and wares of every description consumed or required by the people of the vast territory drained by the Columbia and its tributaries. With convenient wharves and warehouses for reshipping and packing, trade radiates in every direction to supply the extensive mining, agricultural and lumbering districts of the State and surrounding Territories.

The Willamette river is navigable to Portland, at all seasons, for sea going vessels. A line of first-class ocean steamships runs regularly between Portland and San Francisco, making three trips per month, and another line communicates regularly with Victoria, on Vancouver Island, and the different towns on Puget Sound. Portland, by means of sailing vessels, enjoys direct trade with New York, Liverpool, the Sandwich Islands and China, affording advantages for the importation of foreign merchandise and for the exportation to distant markets of Oregon produce.

Portland has a population of about 10,000 inhabitants. Water is supplied to all parts of the town, by means of extensive water works, at low cost, and of the best quality. The streets and public buildings, churches &c., are lighted with gas. The city has five public schools and eight select schools and seminaries. It has sixteen churches, three Masonic associations, four Odd-Fellows' associations, three Lodges of the Good Templars, six Benevolent associations, and a Library of 4,000 volumes. Portland is the headquarters of the Military Department of the Columbia, with its various staff departments, and the United States, Circuit and District Courts, for the district of Oregon, are held here.

The Fire Department of the city consists of 225 active members ;—two steam fire engines, two hand engines, one hook and ladder truck, hose carts, etc. The city has thirty-six cisterns, with a capacity of 600,000 gallons, as a provision against fire. Portland is said to have the best and cleanest streets of any town on the Pacific coast. Its improvements of this kind are : 30,565 square yards of Nicholson pavement; 28,217 linear feet of planked street; 12,040 linear feet of plank gutters; 169,994 linear feet of plank sidewalks. The court house building, Odd Fellows temple, Methodist Church and bank building of Messrs. Ladd & Tilton are structures that would be considered a credit to any city, large or small.

The following table shows the assessed value of the taxable property of the city for the past five years, together with the rate of taxation levied each year.

	Taxable property.	Rate of Tax.
1865	$3,771,575.	12 mills.
1866	4,186,177.	4½ "
1867	4,271,100.	8 "
1868	4,519,061.	9 "
1869	5,144,062.	10 "

The following statistics are condensed from a semi-annual review of the business and commerce of Portland for the latter half of the year 1869, published in the *Daily Oregon Herald*, Jan. 23d, 1870.

Summary of the City Auditor's Report for the year 1869.

In Treasury, January	$14,000 42.	
Receipts.—General fund	39,788 27.	
" Special fund	29,370 62.	
" Street fund	37,469 89.	
		$120,629 20.
Paid.—Warrants.—General fund	$38,136 80.	
" " Special funds	21,486 16.	
" " Street funds	38,201 85.	
" Coupons for interest (special)	2,820 00.	
Loan out, of Building fund	15,000 00.	
On hand, in Treasury, January 1870	4,984 39.	
		$120,629 20.

Shipments of Treasure to San Francisco during the year 1869.

By Wells, Fargo & Co...	$2,559,000 00.
" Ladd & Tilton......................	419,657 30.

Total..	$2,978,657 30.

Internal Revenue Receipts for the District of Oregon, during the six months ending Dec. 31, 1869.

(Collector and Assessor's office at Portland:)

Spirits..................................$22,104 74.		Incomes..............................$110,152 47.
Tobacco............................... 22,660 34.		Legacies.................................. 243 41.
Fermented Liquors................. 4,982 55.		Succession.............................., 760 20.
Banks and Bankers.............. 4,550 56.		Billiard Tables..................... 30 00.
Gross Receipts..................... 7,039 39.		Carriages................................. 713 00.
Sales..................................... 4,263 04.		Silver Plate.......................... 84 70.
Special Taxes...................... 25,567 19.		Watches................................. 1,066 75.
		Gas....................................... 313 83.

Total..............................$204,532 17.

During the six months under review there were recorded at the County Recorder's office 448 Deeds of conveyances of real estate with an aggregate consideration of $599,901 10; and 127 Mortgages with an aggregate amount of loans of $164,130 71, exclusive of a Railroad Mortgage of $2,400,000.

Table—Showing Sales in the City of Portland during six months ending Dec. 31, 1869.

Trade,	No. of Houses.	Total.
Dry goods..	5	$ 941,969
Groceries...............	4	1,225,514
Produce	3	378,279
Tobacco	4	124,188
Brooms.	1	5,505
Liquors..	6	148,657.
Hardware..	4	339,367
Harness and saddles...	3	16,408
Sash, doors and blinds................	3	43,354
Bags and tents...	1	17,712
Confectionary.......................	1	7,968
Carriages and wagons.......................................	1	4.752
Planed lumber ....·.................	2	15,941
Agricultural Implements..............	2	121,975
Boots and shoes...	1	80,109
Bakers, (bread, &c.)..	2	14,879
Pig iron..	1	12,512
Machinery..	3	89,231
Drugs and medicines.................. ....,	2	131,118
Auction sales...	1	76,045
Carpets...	1	49,196
Total	51	$3,842,679.

Consumption of Coal gas...................................,.................3,036,900 cubic-feet.
" " Lumber.................................. ..10,680,000 feet.

Exports to California.

From the Statistics for the year 1869, published in the *Daily Alta California*, we are enabled to compilé the following table, showing the amount of our exports of various products, to the port of San Francisco, from January 1st to December 31st, 1869, both inclusive:

Articles.	No.	Articles.	No.
Barley, sacks............................	240	Beef, barrels........................	1,305
Eggs, cases...............................	10,516	" half barrels...........................	55
Salmon, barrels	3,792	Pork, barrels	965
" half barrels..................	4,746	" half barrels......................	146
" packages.......................	22,130	" gunnies............................	14
Flour, quarter sacks..................	576,280	Bacon, "	593
Apples (dried), barrels.............,	274	" packages·.......................	3,924
" " half barrels.........	3,326	Hams, gunnies...........................	15₃

Apples (dried) kegs.................... 1,926	Bacon, packages........................ 664
" (green) boxes.................. 35,351	Butter, " 1,197
Leather, packages..................... 398	Lard, half barrels...................... 439
Middlings, sacks........................ 7,568	" kegs... 3,151
Oats, sacks... 63,235	Rye, sacks................................ 327
Onions, sacks........................ 1,440	Wheat, sacks 49,360

The receipts of Lumber at San Francisco, during 1868 and 1869, respectively, were as follows :

	1868.	1869.	
From—	*No. feet.*	*No. feet.*	*Increase.*
Columbia river.....................5,481,000.	6,818,547.	1,327,547.

The shipment of wool to San Francisco, in 1869, amounted to 1,039,400 pounds, whilst in 1868, it amounted to only 421,360 pounds ; showing an increase of 617,490 pounds last year.

The foregoing table exhibits the exports to California only. No information is at hand from which a table of the exports to foreign countries can be made. In this connection it may be well to remark that the Willamette valley is the only part of Oregon that exports its produce from Portland; the southern and Eastern part of the State market their produce in other directions, and the lumbering establishments on the coast, ship to San Francisco direct.

Table--Showing the number of Steamers and Sailing Vessels arriving in the Columbia River during the years 1868 and 1869:

	1868.			1869.		
Rig.	*From foreign ports.*	*From native ports.*	*Total.*	*From foreign ports.*	*From native ports.*	*Total.*
Steamers.....	36	39	75	47	45	92
Ships.........	1	...	1	1	2	3
Barks........	1	36	37	2	33	35
Brigs........	...	6	6	2	7	9
Schooners ...	7	6	13	4	12	16
Total......	45	87	132	56	99	155

Summary of Occupations in Portland.

Accountants 59, Attorneys at Law 51, Advertising Agent 1, Assay Office 1, Auctioneer 1, Architect 7, Dealers in Agricultural Implements 3, Banking Houses 4, Barrel Factory 1, Booksellers and Stationers 3, Boot and Shoe Dealers 4, Boot and Shoe Makers 17, Boarding Houses 9, Bakeries 7, Brickyards 2, Broom Factory 1, Barber Saloons 10, Blacksmith's Shops 8, Box Factory 1, Baths 2, Breweries 5, Bookbinderies 2, Brokers 6, Bag Factories 2, Civil Engineers 2, Commission Merchants 11, Contractors 7, Claim Agents 3, Collecting Agents 5, Coppersmith 1, Coffee and Oyster Saloons 3, Clothing Dealers 6. Cigar Makers 2, Confectioners 3, Crockery Dealers 5, Coopers 3, Cheap John store 1. Carver 1, Cigar and Tobacco Dealers 16, Carpets and Paper Hangings 3, Cabinet Makers 2, Clothing Manufactory 1, Chinese Goods 5, Chinese Physicians 3, Dress Makers 17, Drugs and Medicines 7, Dancing Academy 1, Dyer 1, Dentists 4, Express Company 1. Electric Physician 1, Engineers 10, Editors 6, Fish Markets 2, Furrier 1, Foundries 5, Fruit Dealers 5, Furniture Dealers 4, Feed store 1, Gas Works 1, Gas Fitters 3, Gold Dust Dealers 3, Gunsmiths 3, Groceries and Provisions 32, Hair Dressers 2, Hardware Dealers 4, Hat Makers 2, Hotels 14, House and Real Estate Agents 4, Insurance Agents 14, Junk stores 2, Retail Liquor Dealers 47, Wholesale Liquor Dealers 6, Lime and Cement Dealer 1, Dicensed Draymen 13, Livery Stables 12, Leather and Findings 2, Retail Dry Goods Houses 27, Wholesale Dry Goods Houses 8, Lumber Merchants 4, Laundries 4, Match Factory 1, Meat Markets 13, Mills 5, Midwives 2, Milliners 6, Musical Merchandize 2, Musical Instruments 1, Marble and Stone Cutters 2, Notary Public 15, Opticians 2, Ornamental Stucco Work 1, Picture Dealers 2, Produce Dealers 5, Pension Agents 2, Painters 10, Professors of Music 4, Piano Makers 2, Physicians 26, Photograph Galleries 4, Printers (Job-) 2, Publishers of Newspapers, &c., 8, Plummers and Gas Fitters 1, Repackers 2, Real Estate Agents 4, Restaurants 7, Railroad Companies 2, Seed store 1, Sash and Door Factories 2, Salt Works 2, Saddle and Harness Makers 3, Stevedore 1, Stencil Cutter 1, Soda Water Manufacturers 2, Soap Factory 1, Stove and Tinware Dealers 6, Surveyors 2, Sewing Machine Agents 7, Merchant Tailors 6, Telegraph Office 1, Tannery 1, Toy and Fancy Goods Dealers 3, Spice Mill 1, Undertakers 2, Vinegar Manufactory 1, Watch Makers and Jewelers 7, Wagon Materials 1, Wharfinger 1, Wig Maker 1, Wood Dealers 4, Wine and Beer Bottler 1, Writing Teacher 1, Wagon and Carriage Materials 4.

POLK county covers an area of about 1,250 square miles. Population 5,000. Number of voters 1,270. Taxable property $1,518,511. The county has about 100,000 acres of land under ccultivation. It is situated near the center of the Willamette Valley and is one of the best counties in the State. Dallas, the o unty seat, is situated on the Rickreal, a small tributary of the Willamette, and is a flourishing inland town.

TILLAMOOK county, situated on the coast, covers an area of more than 2,000 square miles, but is very sparsely settled. Population 500; acres of land under cultivation 1,500; value of assessable property $59,273. County seat, Lincoln.

UMATILLA county in Eastern Oregon, contains a population of about 2,500. Number of voters, 850. Acres of land under cultivation, about 20,000. Umatilla, the county seat is a place of considerable trade, being the shipping point on the Columbia river from whence supplies are carried inland to the mining regions in eastern Oregon and Idaho. The county has an area of about 6,000 square miles, two thirds of it arable land. Taxable property $790,109.

UNION county is situated in eastern Oregon, and contains within its buondaries large tracts of excellent agricultural and grazing land. Population about 4,000. Number of voters, 1,000. La Grande, the county seat, is situate in the valley of the Grand Ronde, a most fertile region, about 300 miles from Portland. The town contains about 800 inhabitants, a high School and U. S. Land Office. It is located on the main route of travel from the Columbia river to Idaho, and Utah. This county includes the whole of Grand Ronde Valley, containing 288,000 acres of arable land, 15,000 acres under cultivation. Assessable property $768,169.

WASCO county is situated at the Eastern base of the Cascade range. Population about 3,000. Number of voters 609. Asessable property $905,704. Dalles city, the county seat, distant 115 miles from Portland, is a place of considerable trade, all the mershandise intended for eastern Oregon having to pass thorugh it *en route* to its destination. A woolen mill has been put in operation at this point, which will add materially to its progress. The *Mountaineer*, a well conducted weekly newspaper, is published at the Dalles. The United States Government is building a mint at this place. Wasco is one of the best stock raising counties in Oregon.

WASHINGTON county contains a population of about 4,500. Number of voters, 803. Acres of land under cultivation, 25,000. Value of assessable property, $867.265 This county embraces some of the finest agricultural land in the State, and is well settled by thrifty farmers, whose industry is amply rewarded. Hillsboro the county seat, eighteen miles west of Portland, is located upon the Tualatin plains, near a branch of the Tualatin river. This county has an area of 350,000 acres, nearly all arable land. The Pacific University is located at Forest Grove in this county.

YAMHILL county may be classed among the best agricultural portions of the State. It contains a population of 6,000. Number of voters. 1,208. Acres of land under cultivation, 60,000. Value of assessable property, $928,825. Lafayette, the county seat, is located on the left bank of the Yamhill river, thirty miles south-west of Portland. It is annally increasing in business and population. The other towns and post offices are Amity, Muddy, Mountain House, McMinnville, North Yamhill, Sheridan, West Chehalim, and Wheatland. This county raised 600,000 bushels of grain in 1869. The Yamhill river is navigable to McMinnville during high water. The county contains about 500 square miles, nearly all arable land.

MARKET FACILITIES, AND COST OF TRANSPORTATION.

The Columbia River forms the northern boundary of Oregon, and is navigable to the mouth of the Willamette, 100 miles from the sea, at all seasons of the year, for sea-going vessels. Above the Willamette it is navigated by regularly established lines of river steamers, to Wallula, a distince of 240 miles, with two interuptions, one of 6 miles at the Cascades, and one of 14 miles at The Dalles, where portages are made by means of railroads forming connections with the boats. Above Wallula the Columbia and one of its tributaries, the Snake River, is navigated to Lewiston during periods of high water, a point in Idaho Territory at the base of the Bitter Root Mountains, and over 400 miles from the ocean.

The Willamette River is navigable to Portland, 12 miles from its mouth, for ocean steamers and sea-going vessels : and above Portland for river steamers as high as Harrisburg at all seasons, fland during high water as high as Eugene City, a distance of 200 'miles from Portland, by the course of the river. The Yamhill and Tualatin rivers, tributaries to the Willamette, flowing from the west, are navigable during periods of high water to the interior of large agricultural districts situated in Yamhill and Washington Counties.

The business of that part of Oregon drained by these waters engages the services of about thirty river steamboats. All points of the Columbia from The Dalles down, and on the Willamette from Salem down, are in daily communication with Portland. San Francisco is the principal market for the products of the Willamette Valley, although a large trade exists with British Columbia and the lumbering districts of Puget Sound, and cargoes of wheat, flour and other Oregon products are often shipped to the Sandwich Islands, China, Australia, South America, New York and Liverpool, direct from Portland. Farmers, as a rule, dispose of their crops to the mills located in their own neighborhoods, or to dealers in Portland who ship to foreign markets on their own account. The price of most farm products in the Willamette Valley are regulated by the condition of the foreign markets. Those markets, however, are numerous, embracing all the seaport towns in all the countries bordering the Pacific Ocean, so that notwithstanding wheat may be low in Liverpool, it might be high in China; or if low in both these, it still may be high in South America. The outlet to the sea enjoyed by the region of country drained by the Columbia and its tributaries gives it an advantage in this respect over all sections in the interior of a continent.

The following tables exhibit the cost of transportation for all classes of freight on the Willamette River, between four of the principal shipping points in the Valley and Portland, both for produce going down and merchandise going up; and also the rates for the different classes of freight between Portland and San Francisco, and on the Columbia River:

From	Flour per ton.	Wheat per bush.	Oats per bush.	Apples per ton.	Mdse up per ton.
Eugene City to Portland......	$7.50	.22½	.14	$5.00	$14.00
Corvallis " "	5.00	.15	.10	3.00	10.00
Albany " "	4.50	.13½	.09	3.00	9.00
Salem " "	4.00	.12	.08	3.00	7.00

	Mdse.	Flour, Wheat, Oats, Feed per ton.
Portland to San Francisco, Steamer..........	$6.00	4.00
Sailing vessel...	3.75	3.75
San Francisco to Portland, Steamer..........	8.00	
Sailing vessel...	4.00	

Cost of Transportation on the Columbia.

	1st class.	2d class.	3d class.
From Portland to the Dalles	$15.00	$12.50	$10.00
Umatilla	25.00	20.00	15.00
Wallula	30.00	25.00	20.00
Lewiston	50.00	40.00	30,00
Through bills of lading from San Francisco to Umatilla	30.50	25.50	20.50

The freighting business on the lower Columbia is confined to lumber and fish principally, as farming is carried on along the river only to a small extent. The freight on lumber to San Francisco from all points below the mouth of the Willamette is $6 per M. feet, and on other commodities the same as from Portland. The marketing facilities for the valley of the Willamette will be very much enlarged in the course of two or three years, by the completion of two lines of railway now in course of construction and extending from Portland south, one on each side of the valley, thus making three channels of communication through the valley to Portland—the river in the center and a railroad on each side. Twenty miles of the road on the eastern side is now in operation, and twenty miles of the one on the west side has been graded; both are to be pushed forward vigorously.

The Umpqua valley has less advantages in the way of markets for produce than the Willamette. Although the river is navigated for a short distance, and affords a means of access for goods and merchandise to supply the wants of the people, yet as a route of transportation for getting to market heavy crops, it has thus far proved insufficient. Improvements, however, are being made in the river, and with the expenditure of some capital in that way the facilities for getting the crops of the Umpqua to sea will be very much improved. Rogue River valley is situated still farther from the sea-board than the Umpqua, and being entirely without navigable water of any kind, its only market is amongst the mining population in that part of Oregon and Northern California. The mines, however, furnish a good market as far as it goes. They have been sufficient to build up quite large and prosperous communities in the farming districts depending on them. Stock-raising has become the principal reliance of these two valleys in Southern Oregon. Stock dealers from California, Nevada and Idaho visit them regularly every year and buy up the surplus of all kinds, paying cash for it, thus giving the farmer a market at his own door for everything that can be driven away. His bacon and wool, of which the product is quite large, can be sent to market much easier than heavy grain crops when transportation is expensive. Douglas county in the year 1869 realized from the sale of its surplus live stock, bacon and wool, $600,000 in gold. The people of Coos and other counties, situated in the southwestern part of the State, on the coast, transact their business entirely with San Francisco. Coos Bay is the principal harbor; lumber and coal the principal exports. Farmers in this neighborhood have a home market for their produce, and notwithstanding the richness of the soil and the large amount of farming land, the area under cultivation is so small that the coal mines and lumbering establishments import every year large quantities of flour to supply their wants.

In Eastern Oregon, the farmers have a home market in their own mining camps and new settlements, and those of the Territories of Idaho and Montana. Consequently prices rule higher than in Western Oregon, excepting live stock, in which there is very little if any difference. The distance from the sea-board makes it somewhat expensive to market a crop in that direction. But owing to the large number of persons employed in the mines, and the small number of farmers, there is very rarely a surplus of farm products. Live stock finds a market not only in the mining districts, but in the surrounding States and Territories and in British Columbia.

MARKET REPORTS, COST OF LIVING, &c.

(From the *Daily Oregon Herald*, March 15, 1870.)
Wholesale and Jobbing Prices Current at Portland.
GROCERIES AND PROVISIONS.

Alcohol—$2 35.

Beans—White 3½@4 c; Red 3½; Pink 3½; Bayos, 4; Butter 4.

Candles—Adamantine Harkness' 22c; Grant's 19 @ 19½; Gross' 18; Emery's 18@18½; Schmidt's 18@18½; Macy's 18@18½; Patent Sperm 45@50; Parafein 35.

Cider—Harrington's ⅌ gal. 75c; Jackson's 75c.

Coffee—Costa Rica 20½@21; Java 25@26; Rio 19½@20; Kona 19.

Cream Tartar—Hunnewell's 50c; Donelly's 45c; Venard's 45 @ 50 c; Smith & Davis' 52c.

Farina—3@3¼.

Fish—Cod, Pacific, 11½; Eastern 15; Dessicated Cod per ℔ 30c; Mackerel No. 1 per hf bbl $16 75; do. No. 1 per kit 4 25; do. No. 1 mess per kit, 4 75. Salmon pickled hf bbl 5 50, bbl 9 50. Sardines qrs $2@2¾; hfs 3 25@3 75.

Fruits (dried) *and Preserves*—Apples 4½@5½c; Peaches, new, 11 @ 12½c. Hungarian Prunes 14@15 c. Raisins, boxes, $4 50; half boxes 4 75; quarter boxes 5. Zante Currants 17; Oregon do. 10@12. Citron 40. Peaches fresh, in tins, 4¼@4¾. Jams $5 50. Assorted Pie Fruits 4 25. Table Fruits 4 00@4 25. Jellies, in tins, 5 50. Honey, in tins, 4 50. Green Corn, in tins, 3 50@4 00. Green Peas, in tins, 4 25@4 75. Clams, in tins, 4 50. Lobsters, in tins, 3 50 @ 3 75. Oysters, Field's, 3 50; McMurry's 3 75; Myer's 3 75; other brands 3 25@3 50.

Hominy—6@6½.

Maccaroni—No. 1, 2 50; No. 2, 2 00.

Matches—California 2 00; Oregon 1 87½@2 00; Parlor 3 75.

Molasses and Syrups—Hawaiian Molasses 25 cents; do. Syrup, in kegs, 40 cents; Syrup, Pacific, 82½@87½, do. in hf bbls 77½@82½; do. bbls 72½a77½ c; California extra heavy golden syrup, kegs, 90a92½ c; do. bbls 77½a82½ c.

Nuts—Almonds 30a35 c; English Walnuts 12½a14; Brazil 20; Filberts 20 c; Peanuts 16 c; Pecon 30 c;

Oils—Olive 5 50a9 50, Linseed 1 15a1 20; Sperm 2 50; Whale 60a90 c; Lard 1 85: Devoes', Downer's, Pratt's, other brands, Coal, 52½a55 c.

Pickles—California, hf gals., 4 75a5 00; quarts 3 25; English, quarts, 3 50.

Peas, split, 7½ c.

Pearl Barley—No. 1, 10 c; No. 2, 8 c.

Provisions—Mess Beef pr bbl $18 00; Mess Pork 24 00; Hams, 13a15 c; do. sugar cured (Cross') 25 c, (Smith, Brasfield & Co's.) 20 c; Shoulders, 7a8 c; do. sugar cured (Cross') 11 c; Bacon, clear side, 13½a14 c; Lard, in tins, 13a15; do., in barrels, 12½a13 c. Butter, choice, 20 c; do., ordinary to fair, 16a18 c. Cheese, California, 22 c; do. Eastern 24 c; do. Oregon 18 c; Eggs 20 c.

Rice—China 6¼a6½. Patna 7½a8 c. Hawaiian, 9a10 c. Batavia 6½a7 c.

Saleratus—Babbit's 11 c. Barton's 9a9½ c.

Salt—Liverpool $42 50a45 00; Carmen Island 32 50a35 00; Bay 21 00; Ground Rock 21 00a22 50; San Quentin 30 00.

Sago—12½a15 c.

Sauces—Worcestershire, pts, 7 00 a 7 50; do. hf pts, 4 50a4 75; Tomato Catsup, pts, 1 75; qts 2 25; Capers 4 50a5 00; Pepper sauce 2a2½.

Soap—Castile, 16a17 c. Chemical Olive 1 45a1 60. California, pale, 1 50. Oregon 1 40 a 1 50.

Soda—Babbit's 11. Barton's 9½. Sal. 4½a5. Bi-Carb. kegs, 8 c.

Spices—Cloves 50 c; Cassia 62½a70 c; Nutmegs 1 25a1 37½; Mace 1 40a1 50; Pepper, Grain, 30a32 c; Mustard, Cal., 1 40a1 62½; do. French, 2 50a2 75. Pepper, ground, 1 50a1 75; do. Cayenne 1 75. Allspice, ground, 1 50a1 75; do. grain, 30 c. Ginger, ground, 1 50a1 75.

Starch—Glenfield 19½a20. Corn, 15a[illegible]. Duryea's 15 c; Pearl 12½. Oswego, Kingsford's 10½a13½.

Sugars—Crushed. bbls, 15½; half bbls 15¾; pulverized, boxes, 16½; kegs 16¾ c; granulated 14½a15c; yellow C. ref. bbls, 12½a12¾c; kegs 12¾a13c; Hawaiian 8½a11c; China none.

Tapioca—12½a15.

Teas—Young Hyson 1 00a1 50; Gunpowder and Imperial 1 25; Black 55ca1 00; Japan 80a90c.

Vermicelli—2 00a2 50.

Vinegar—California 47½; Oregon 30c.

Yeast Powders—Preston & Merrill's $26 00; Donnolly's 25 00.

Wood and Willow Ware, per nest—Pails, painted, 3 00a3 50, do. Cedar 4 50a5 00. Tubs, painted, 4 00a4 50; do. Cedar 5 50. Brooms, Oregon No. 1, 6 25; No. 2 5 25; No. 3 4 25. California No. 1, 5 50a6 00; No. 2, 4 50a5 00; No. 3, 3 50a4 00.

PRODUCE.

Feed, &c.—Corn Meal per 100 3 50. Ground Feed per ton, 25 00. Bran 13 00. Middlings 22 00a25 00.

Flour—Extra 4 50a5 00. Superfines 4 00. Fine 3 75.

Fruits (Green)—Apples 1 00a1 50 per box. Pears 50ca1 00. Plums none. Peaches none.

Grain—Wheat, white, 70a75c; red 70c. Barley ℔ 100 ℔s 1 25. Oats ℔ bbl 40a45c. Corn ℔ bushel 1 00. Beans 3½a5c.

Hay—Bailed ℔ ton 12 00; Loose 11 00.

Onions ℔ ℔ 2½c.

Potatoes—Cal., none. Oregon ℔ bushel 40a50c.

MISCELLANEOUS.

Agricultural Implements.—Haines' Headers $325 00. Sweepstake Tresher 500 00 to 800 00. Buckeye Mowers 140 00 to 160 00. Buckeye Mower & Reaper combined 225 00. Buckeye Grain Drill 120 00. "Sattleys" and Skinner's Gang Plows 80 00a 90 00. Cast-steel Plows 19 00a20 00. "Moline," "Peoria,", "Galena", "Chicago" and "Boston Clipper" Steel Plows 14 00a18 00. Breaking Plows 25 00a40 00. Cultivators, various kinds, 10 00a19 00. Garden barrows, 8 00a10 00. Wescott's Pat. Churns, 8 00a16 00. Bains' Wisconsin made Farm Wagons, with double box, brake, &c., &c., 175 00a185 00.

Bags and Bagging—Burlap Bags 22x36 ea 12c; do. 23x40 13c; Dundee Gunnies 16½c. Linen, for Flour Bags, none. Burlap, ℔ yard, 10½c

Cement, &c.—New Jersey 5 00. Astoria 4 50. Calcine plaster 5 00. Land plaster 3 50. Santa Cruz Lime 2 75. San Juan Lime 2 50a2 75.

Cigars—Havana per M $115 00a200 00. Swiss 22 00a35 00. Domestic 20 00a90 00.

Drugs—Alum, bbls 6c. Borax Eastern 40a45c. Blue Vitriol 13c. Potash Ganiz 1 ℔ can, per doz., 2 25. Rosin per bbl 8 00a12 00. Saltpetre, kegs, 16a25c. Sulphur 8½a12½c.

Dry Goods—Standard Drills 16½a17½. Seconds Drills 14a14½. Sheetings, Standard, 14½a15½; do. medium 13½a14; do. light 12½a13. Houselining, 9½a10; do Blea. ⅞, 7½ a 9; do. ⅞, 10½a13½; do. 4-4, 13½a20. Cotton checks 15a25; Linen 25½a27. Cambrics 10½a11½. Cotton Flannel, blea, 16½a22; do. brown 15a20. Cottonades, light, 25a 30; do. heavy, 37½a50. Denims 15a25. Hickory Stripes 15a25. Prints, Standard, 11a12; do. seconds, 9½a10. Linseys, 20a37½. Ticks ⅞, 16½a22; do. 4-4, 25a35. Bear Duck 27. Table Damasks, brown, 37½a62½; bleac. 50a87½. Diaper Linen 37½a50. Seamless sacks 37½a45. Alpacas, blk, 27½a75. Water-proof Cloth 95a1 25. Crash 11½a15.

Gunpowder, &c.—Dupont's, Hazard's and California, Rifle Powder, 1 ℔ cans, 55c; ½℔ 65 c; Eagle Duck No. 1, 2 and 3, per ¼ keg 4 50: hf keg 8 50. Blasting powder per keg 2 75; Valley Mills, 1 ℔ cans, 50c; ½ ℔ 60c. Dupont's Fuse, Double Tape, ℔ M $18 00, single 15 00.

Hardware—Hunt's Axes, per doz., $15 00a16 00; do. handled, 18 00. long handled Shovels 12 00a13 50. Ames & Ray's Shovels 16 50. Spades, long handled, 15 00a 18 00; do. D. H., 13 00a18 00. Hay Forks, two tine, 7 00a9 00; do. three tine, 10 50 a13 50. Manure Forks 14 00a15 00. Garden Hoes 9 00. Garden Rakes 10 00a14 50 Spading Forks 15 00a20 00. Nails, cut, 5½c; do. wrought, 9c. Apple Pearers, Lightning and Turntable, 10 00.

Hides—Dry ℔ ℔ 10a11c; green, salted, 6 c; Deer Skins, 16a18c.

Leather.—Oregon, sole, ℔℔ 23a24 c. Harness 28a30 c. Skirting 29a31. Bridle, ℔ doz.., $36a42. Collar $27a30. Calfskins $24a36. Kipskins $45a57. Half Kips, or Wax Leather $27a33. Sheepskins 2 50a5 00. Topping 7 50a9 00, Santa Cruz, Sole, ℔ ℔ 26a28c. French: Calf Skins, ℔ doz., $48a84. Kip Skins $75a96. Topping and Lining Skins $11a12. Buckskins ℔ ℔, 60ca1 00.

Lumber—Redwood boards and ceiling, ℔ M feet, $50; in quantities over three M 47 50. Eastern Lumber, Oak, Hickory and Ash Plank, 16a20c. per foot. Street Plank 12 00. Sidewalk 12 00a13 00. Assorted Rough 14 00a16 00; do. edged 18 50; dressed one side 22 00a23 50; do. two sides 28 50; do, four sides 33. Spruce ceiling and shelving 31. White Fir do. 31. Flooring—Tongued and Grooved 26 00a28 50; do. Dressed two sides 31 00; do. Seasoned 31 00; do. do. Dressed two sides 36 00. Cedar fence posts, rough, 26 00; do. dressed 31 00. Lattice, ℔ linear feet, ¾c. Picketing do. ¾c. Lath ℔ M 3 00. Shingles 2 50. Slab-wood ℔ load 1 50.

Metals—Iron; Scotch and English pig, per ton, none. Refined bar ℔ ℔ 4½c; Sheet, 14 to 20, 7½c; do. 24 to 27, 9c. Oregon pig $41 00 at works. Copper: Sheathing ℔ ℔ 39c; do. yellow 39c; do. bronze 50c; do. old 15½c. Tin Plates: Plates Charcoal, IX per box 14 50; Plates IC char 13 00; Roofing Plates 12 50; Banca Tin slabs ℔ ℔ 48c. Steel: English cast steel ℔ ℔ 18c. Lead: pig ℔ ℔ 9 c; sheet 14c; pipe 13c; bar 12c. Zinc: sheets ℔ ℔ 14c; babbit metal 30a50. Quicksilver 65c.

Oregon Woolen Goods—Blankets, No. 1, 9 00; No. 2, 6 50; No. 3, 5 25; No. 4, 4 50. No. 1, Indian stripe, 7 75; No. 2 do., 7 00. Gray 4 pt 5 75; do. 3 pt 4 75; do. 3 pt blk borders 3 75. Vicuna 4 pt 7 25; do. 3 pt 5 50. Green 4 pt 7 75; do. 3 pt 5 75. Blue 4 pt 7 25; do. 3 pt 5 50. Scarlet 4 pt 8 50; do. 3 pt 6 50. Travelling 8 00a10 00. Family, extra white, 14 00; No. 1, 8 50; No. 2, 7 00; No. 3, 5 50. White Flannels, 37½a50c; plain ass. col'd, 40 c; twilled ass. col'd 45a50c; Blue mixed 37½@45c; Fancy checked 40c; Hard times 90c; Doeskins, blk and col'd 1 00; Fancy cass. 1 00@1 25. Tweeds 65c; Yarns 1 00a1 25; Oregon Shaker Socks 4 50. Terms, 90 days, less 3 ℔ cent. for cash.

Rope—19c.

Seeds—Red Clover 22½a25c. White Clover 75ca1 00. Alfalfa Clover 22½a25c. Orchard Grass 25a30c. Blue Grass 65a75c. Timothy 16a17c. Red Top 40a50c.

Spirits—Whisky: Fine Bourbon, 2 50a4 50; Domestic 1 25a2 00; Scotch and Irish 4 00a5 00. Brandy: French 4 00a15 00; Domestic 2 00a3 50. Gin: Holland 4 50@ 5 00; Domestic 1 50 and upwards. Rum: Jamaica 4 50a5 00; Santa Cruz 4 50a5 00; Domestic 1 50 and upwards. Pure Spirits 90ca1 25. Spirits vary in price according to quality; the above quotations give the range.

Tobacco—Half ℔s Western ℔ ℔ 65a70c; hf ℔s Virginia 65a75c; pounds 12 inches hard pressed 70ca1 00; do. extra choice 1 00a1 10; 9 in. light pressed 80ca1 00; Anderson's solace chewing 11; Solar fine cut 11; Welcome, chewing plain 11; do. rolls 11. Young America, fine cut 11; Cable Twist chewing 85ca1 00 ℔ ℔; Dwarf Twist 95ca1 00 ℔ ℔; Navy ¼, 1-5, ½, ℔, 70a75c ℔ ℔.

Farmers' Price Current.

The following are the prices paid to Farmers for goods purchased from the wagon, &c.:

Produce—Apples, green, ℔ box, 75ca$1 00; do. dried, in kegs, ℔ ℔, 4a4½ cents; Pears, green, ℔ box, 75ca 1 00. Wheat, new white, ℔ bushel, 65a70; do. red, 60a65; Oats 40 c; Corn Meal, W. W., ℔ 100 ℔s, 4 00; do. country, 3 50; Ground Feed, ℔ ton 20 00a25 00; Peaches, dried, ℔ ℔ 8c; Beans ℔ 100 ℔s, 3 00a3 50; Hay, baled, ℔ ton 10 00a11 00; do. from wagons, 10 00; Corn ℔ bushel 1 00; Bran 10 00a12 00; Middlings 18 00a25 00; Onions 1½c ℔ ℔; Potatoes 40c.

Provisions—Bacon ⅌ ℔ 12¼a13; Hams 13c; Shoulders 6a7c; Lard, in tins, 12½c; do. in kegs, 11c; Eggs ⅌ doz. 20c; Butter 18a20c; Chickens, young, ⅌ doz. 5 2½; do. grown, ⅌ doz. 5 50.

Wool, Hides and Furs—Wool ⅌ ℔ 18a20c; Hides, salted, ⅌ ℔ 6 c; do. dry, 9a 11c. Furs: Fisher 1 50a3 00; Fox, cross, 1 00a3 00; do. red 75ca1 00; Martin, prime, dark 2 50a6 00; do. pale, 1 00a2 50; Mink, dark, northern, 25ca1 25; pale 25ca1 00; Muskrat 10c; Otter, prime dark, 1 75a3 50: Sea Otter 25 00a40 00; Coon 12½c; Wolf, black, 1 50a2 00; do. gray; 80ca1 00; Wild Cat 25c; Skunk 12½; Fur Seal 1 50a2 50; Beaver, dark, ⅌ ℔ 75a80c; Bear, black, 2 00a5 00; do. Brown, 2 00a2 50; Cat 25c. *Knit Socks*—⅌ doz. 4 00.

Cattle Market.

Beef Cattle on foot 6a7c.　Mutton Sheep ⅌ head 2 50a3 00.　Fat Hogs, neat ⅌ ℔ 6a6½c.　Stock Hogs, gross 4c.　Veal Calves, neat per ℔ 7a8c.

Retail Family Market.

Green Fruit—Apples ⅌ box $1 00@1 50.　Peeaclis none.　Plums none.　Oranges ⅌ doz 1 00; Limes ⅌ doz. 50c; Cocoanuts 12½@25c each.　Pears 1 00@1 25 ⅌ box; Grapes none; Cranberries 1 00 per gallon; Lemons 1 00 ⅌ doz.　Pine Apples 1 50 each.
Dried Fruits—Figs, California, ⅌ ℔ 25c; do. Asia Minor 33½@37½c.　Apples 10c.. Plums with pits 14@16 c.; do. without 25 c.　Prunes 20@35c.　Pears 10@12½c.　Peaches 12½@16¾.
Groceries—Coffee, ground, ⅌ ℔ 30, 35@40c; do. Costa Rica 25c; do. Java 28@30c.　Sugar, crushed, 20c; do. pulverized 20c; do. granulated 20c; do. yellow, California Sugar Refinery, 16¾c; do. Island No. 1, 16c; do. do. No. 2, 12@13 c.　Heavy Golden Syrup $1 00; Syrup ⅌ gal. 1 12½.　Teas: Young Hyson, first quality 1 50; second do. 1 25; Old yson 1 0 @1 25; black 75c@[00; Comet 1 25; Japan 1 00@1 25.　Condensed Milk ⅌ ℔ 50c.　Candles. ⅌ ℔, Adamantine 25c; Parafine 37½c; Sperm 50c.
Provisions—Butter, choice, 40@50c; do. ordinary to fair, 30@33, common 20@25c.　Cheese, Cal., 30c. do. Eastern 37½c; do. Oregon, 25@33½c.　Hams, farmers' 16@18; Levy's 20; Johnson's 25 c; Cross' 27c; Shoulders, sugar cured, 12½, do. farmers cut, 10.　Bacon. clear side, 16c; do. breakfast 20c.　Eggs ⅌ doz. 25c.　Lard, pure leaf, tins, 1 @17½, do good white 15@17½; do. bulk 15@17½.　Honey, yellow comb. 15@20c; do. white 20 a 25c; Flour, Standard, Imperial, Vaughn's, McLennns, and Salem, per bbl $5 50; per sack 1 50; Centerville 4 25@4 50; North Yamhill 4 25@4 50.
Canned Goods.　Oysters per 2 ℔can 37½@50c; do. 1 ℔can 25c; Lobsters per 2 ℔can 37½@; do. 1 ℔can 25; Clams 50c; Sardines per can 25c; do. hf can 37½c; Green Corn 50c; Green Peas 37½c; Green Beans 37½c; Tomatoes 2 @37½; Peaches 50c; Pine Apple 50c; Strawberries 50c; Blackberries 50c; Apricots 40@50c; Jellies (Cutling's) in tins 60@75c, do. in glass 37½c; Jams in tins 62½c.
Sauces and Pickles.　Worcestershire, (Lea & Perrin's) 50 a 75; do. (Cutting's) 37½c; Tomato Catsup 25 a 37½; Mushroom Catsup 50 c; Capers 37½ a 50c; Curry Powders 50c; French Mustard 37½; Assorted Pickles 25 a 62½; Gherkins 25 a 50c.
Poultry &c.　Chickens ⅌ pair 1 25; Fowls grown 1 25; Ducks ⅌ pair, tame. 1 00 a 1 25; Geese ⅌ pair, tame, 2 00 a 2 50; Turkeys 1 50 a 2 50; Pacific Cod ⅌ ℔ 12½ a 16¾c; Sturgeon 4c; Salmon 8c; Dessicated Cod ⅌ ℔ 45 a 50c.
Vegetables.　Cabbage ⅌ doz. $2 00 a 3 00; Beets 2c; Onions 2½ a 4c; Carrots 2c; Turnips 2c; Garlick 20 a 25c; Potatoes 60 a 75 ⅌ bushel; Sweet Potatoes 5c; Tomatoes none; Parsnips ⅌ ℔ 3 a 4c; Celery 1 50 a 2 00; Cucumber none.　Green Onions ⅌ doz. 75.　Green Corn, none.
Nuts.　Almonds 40 a 50c; Walnuts 20 a 25c; Brazil 37½c; Filberts 37½c; Peanuts 37½c; Pecan 37½; Ceestnuts 75c; Hickory 37½c.
Meats.　Beef ⅌ ℔ 10 a 12½c; do. choice, cut, 15 a 18c; Mutton 12½c; Veal 15c; Pork 12½c.
Firewood. Fir, long, $4 00; do. sawed 5 00; do. sawed and split 5 75; Ash, long, 5 a 5 50; do. sawed 6 00 a 6 50; do. sawed and split 7 00 a 7 50; Oak, Dogwood and Vine Maple, long, 6 0; sawed 7 00; do. sawed and split 7 50 a 8 00.

The average cost of an army ration in the Department of the Columbia for the year 1869, was a fraction over 21¼ cents, the supplies being purchased in Oregon and Washington Territory.

RENTS IN PORTLAND.—Dwellings of eight or nine rooms, hard finished, with cellar, out-houses, water and all necessary conveniences, $25 to $40 per month, according to locality; dwelling of six rooms, hard finished, &c., &c., $16 to $25 per month; tenement houses of six rooms, papered, $12; tenements of four rooms $8. Building lots 50x100 feet, in good situations, sell at from $1,000 to $1,500; building lots of the same size in the back part of town, $100 to $250. The cost of erecting a dwelling, one and a half story, with six rooms hard finished, cellar, cistern, out-houses and fences would amount to $1,500 or $2,000.

In the interior towns the cost of building lots and the range of rents for dwellings is much lower, while the cost of buildings, depending a good deal on the price of labor, would vary but little from the above. Board at the principal hotels, in Portland is furnished at $6 per week; board and lodging (room furnished) $10; at the cheap hotels and boarding houses, mechanics and laboring men obtain board at $4,50 to $5 per week; board and lodging $5 50 and $6. In the towns of the Willamette Valley the general cost of living is a little under that of Portland, if there is any difference; while in Eastern Oregon it is considerably over it, particularly in the mining districts.

The following are quotations of leading articles of produce and provisions at La Grande, Eastern Oregon, on the 19th of March: Dried Apples, 14a16c. Hams, 25a30c. Bacon, 20a23c. Shoulders, 18a20c. Lard in tins, 25c. Butter, choice, 45c; ordinary to fair, 30a37½. Eggs, fresh, 25c. Feed—none in the market. Flour, extra, per bbl, $11; superfine,$10; fine, $9. Wheat, fair, $1 25; extra, for seed, $1 50. Oats, per lb, 2c. Onions, per lb, 4a6c.

PRICE OF FARMING LANDS.

In Western Oregon farms are of large size, generally 640 acres—often twice that much—a natural result of the policy adopted by the General Government towards the early settlers. The settlements of the Willamette valley cover an area about equal to the State of Connecticut, but its population is only about 75,000 or 80,000. As a matter of course, only a small proportion of the land is under cultivation. Land is cheap because there is so much of it in proportion to population. To furnish the data from which an estimate may be made of the average price of farming lands, recourse is had to the books of the Board of Immigration, and of a prominent firm of real estate agents in Portland.

On the books in the office of the Board of Immigration there are twenty-five farms offered for sale, at prices ranging as follows: One at $25 per acre; three at $20; one at $19 25; one at $14 25; one at $13; one at $12; two at $11 50; one at $10; two at $9 50; two at $9 25; three at $7 50; one at $6 66; two at $6; one at $5 75; two at $4 50; one at $3 50; average, $10 94. The books of the real estate agents exhibit twenty farms for sale in Multnomah county, at an average price of $11 per acre, and twenty in Clackamas county, at an average of $8 per acre; highest price, $27 50; lowest, $3. In Yamhill county the same firm has ten farms for sale at an average price of $7 per acre; highest, $18; lowest, $4; and in Washington county they have forty-two farms, at an average rate of $7 50 per acre. The above figures represent the value of farming lands in the northern and central part of the Willamette valley as nearly as it is possible to arrive at it. Unimproved, timbered lands, throughout the same region are held at from $1 25 to $4 per acre, except immediately around the city of Portland, and perhaps some other towns, where the rapid growth of the town and increasing value of town property gives a value to adjacent lands for homestead and other purposes, much higher than for mere farming purposes. The wide range in the prices of the foregoing list is to be attributed mainly to difference in improvements. Of course, costly improvements add very much to the rate per acre, while a farm with cheap and temporary improvements is offered at a price but little if any above the value of wild land. The distance from navigable water and facilities for marketing are also considerations that go to make up the value of a farm. No data is at hand from which to get an average of the price of land in other parts of Oregon, but it is confidently believed that nowhere will it exceed the prices embraced in the foregoing list, and in most places it will fall below it.

GOVERNMENT LANDS.

The large valleys of Western Oregon were settled at first under the donation laws of 1850, which gave to each man of a family 640 acres of land, and to every single man 320 acres, in consideration of occupancy and cultivation for a period of years. This law expired in 1854, but was in force long enough for the finest lands in Western Oregon to be taken by the settlers under its provisions. The pre-emption and homestead laws of the United States were afterwards extended and applied to Oregon, which enabled subsequent settlers to obtain 160 acres each, so that the prairie lands of the three principal valleys are at the present time about all occupied. The rates at which these lands can now be purchased from the present occupants are given in another place in this pamphlet. While such are the leading facts relative to the prairie lands of the valleys, there are still good government lands to be had among the foot-hills each side of the valleys, and on the slopes of the mountain ranges. These slopes and valleys are more or less timbered, the uplands generally with fir, pine and cedar, and the valleys and creek bottoms with a growth of ash, alder, maple and underbrush. The quality of the lands even on the high ridges is superior to the average farming lands of New England, and on the bottoms it is equal to any land in the world. The amount of land of this doscription, in Western Oregon, still vacant and subject to be taken under the homestead and pre-emption laws, is greater than that comprised within the whole State of Massachusetts. There are several localities near the coast where several hundred families could settle in a body, on lands of the best quality, in a section and climate adapted to the growth of all classes of farm products, except corn.

In Eastern Oregon the amount of government land still vacant is very large. The section of country known as the Klamath lake region, in the southwestern corner of Eastern Oregon, is as large as the State of Rhode Island. About half of it is the finest kind of arable prairie land, the remainder good grazing and timber lands—all well watered. This entire section of country does not now contain over forty or fifty settlers. In the northern part of Eastern Oregon is a strip of high, rolling prairie land, ten or fifteen miles wide, skirting the northern base of the Blue Mountains, and extending from the Cascade Mountains to the eastern line of the State, a distance of one hundred and fifty miles. It is reasonably well watered; timber convenient on the adjacent mountains, and well adapted to grain growing, grazing and dairying purposes. Its present number of settlers is very small. Vacant lands in large quantities are still to be obtained in Grande Ronde, John Day's, Harney Lake and Deschutes valleys, in addition to which there are hundreds of small valleys distributed throughout the vast territory known as Eastern Oregon, containing bottom land of the finest quality for farming, and hill and table land unsurpassed for stock-raising purposes.

The great majority of the vacant lands in Eastern Oregon still belong to the government. The exceptions are, in the case of the State of Oregon, which has located several large tracts under acts of Congress granting lands for certain specific purposes and grants given to two different military road companies, of alternate sections for three miles each side of their respective roads. The land enuring to the roads under these grants is private property and will be sold at whatever it will bring; that belonging to the State is for sale, under an act of the Legislature, at $2 per acre, and the reserved sections of government lands within the limits of the wagon road grants are subject to homestead settlement, at the rate of 80 acres to each settler. All other government lands can be taken at the rate of one quarter section, or one hundred and sixty acres to each settler.

PRE-EMPTION AND HOMESTEAD LAWS OF THE UNITED STATES.

"PRE-EMPTIONS."—Every person, being the head of a family, or widow or single man over the age of twenty-one years, and being a citizen of the United States or who shall have declared his intentions to become a citizen, is allowed by law to make a settlement on any public land of the United States not appropriated or reserved. In the case of unsurveyed lands 'legal inception' by actual settlement will take place, but no proceeding toward completion of title can be had until after the land has been surveyed and the surveys returned to the District Land Office. The settler is obliged to erect a dwelling, occupy and improve the land and make it his or her home. But no person can obtain the benefit of more than one pre-emption right, and no person who is the owner of 320 acres of land in any State or Territory, or who shall abandon his residence on his own land, to live on the public land, can acquire any right of pre-emption. Where the tract on which settlement is made has once been *offered* at public sale, a declaratory statement as to the fact of settlement must be made at the Land Office within thirty days from the date of settlement, and within one year from that date, proof of residence and cultivation must be made and the land paid for. Where the tract has been surveyed but *not* offered at public sale, the claimant must file his statement within three months from the date of settlement, and make proof and payment before the day designated by the President for the public sale of the lands.

The quantity of land allowed to one settler by pre-emption, is one quarter section, or 160 acres, and the price to be paid, is $1 25 per acre, except in the case of *alternate* sections embraced in any railroad reservation, which is $2 50 per acre.

Should the settler die before establishing his claim within the period limited by law, the title may be perfected by the executor, administrator or one of the heirs, by making the requisite proof of settlement and paying for the land.

In the case of a settlement made on *unsurveyed* lands, the claimant must file notice of settlement within three months after the receipt of the township plat at the District Land Office, and make proof and payment as required in the case where surveys had been made previous to settlement.

"HOMESTEADS." The Homestead Law gives to every citizen

of the United States or foreigner declaring his intention to become such, the right to a homestead on *surveyed* lands. This is conceded to the extent of one quarter section, or 160 acres, of land not embraced within the limits of railroad or other reservation, or 80 acres, when the location is made on alternate sections embraced *within* such reserves. To obtain homesteads the party must make affidavit that he is the head of a family, or, a single man over twenty one years of age, that he is a citizen or has declared his intention to become one, and that the location is made for his exclusive use and benefit for actual settlement and cultivation. The fees and expenses connected with the loca tion of a homestead in Oregon are $22,00 when the full amou of land is taken, or $11,00 if half the quantity all d located. On making the affidavit before the R ment of the fees, a duplicate receipt w an inceptive right in the settler, and u the law, which requires continuous set for the period of five years, and upon pro fact to the Land officers within two years after s expired, certificates will be issued as a basis of a c te title to the land.

Where a homestead settler dies before the consummation of his claim, the heirs may continue the settlement and obtain upon requisite proof at the proper time.

A homestead settler cannot sell his claim until after is complete, but he can at any time relinquish his rendering his receipts, after which he is not allow other settlement under the homestead law.

A settlement made under the pre-emption law may to a homestead entry, if no adverse right intervenes.

If the Homestead settler does not wish to remain five years on his tract, the law permits him to pay for it with cash, at the prescribed rates for claims taken by pre-emption, and upon proof of settlement and cultivation from date of entry to time of payment.

Lands obtained under the Homestead laws are exempt from liability for debts contracted prior to the issuing of a complete title by the government.

Another method of obtaining government lands is by " private entry " and applies only to such lands as have been *offered* at public sale and remain unsold. In this case payment in cash or land warrants can be made at once and a complete title obtained without delay, other than the time necessary to transmit the papers to the General Land Office and receive the patent in return. The price of land at "private entry" is $1,25 per acre, except in the case of reserved sections; that is $2,50 per acre. At cash entry any quantity can be taken that is desired. In Eastern Oregon there is no land subject to "private entry" but there is a large amount of it in Western Oregon.

There are three Land Offices in Oregon for the transaction of business connected with the disposal of government lands ; one at Oregon City, in the Willamette Valley ; one at Roseburg, in the Umpqua Valley, and one at LaGrande in Grand Ronde Valley.

STOCK RAISING.

The facilities which exist in Oregon for raising stock have been mentioned heretofore in connection with the soil and climate. But in order to illustrate those facilities more clearly, reference is had to the statistics of the Government contained in the census reports of 1860 ; and a comparison drawm between the cost of raising stock in Oregon, on the Northwest coast, and in Maine, on the Northeast coast of the United States, both States being situated in about the same latitude. Maine produced in 1860, 975,716 tons of hay, feeding 890,148 head of stock, embracing horses, cattle and sheep. Oregon the same year produced 26,441 tons of hay, feeding 267,025 head of stock. The average consumption of hay for each animal in Maine was 2,197 pounds, against 197 pounds consumed in Oregon. Estimating the hay to be worth $6 per ton, the cost of wintering an animal in Maine was $6 59 ; in Oregon 59 cents, a difference of $6 per head. The animals in Maine were worth $15,437,533, or $17 34 each. The stock in Oregon was worth $6,272,892, or $23 49 each ; a difference of $6 15 per head, to which add the difference of $6 for feed, and the result is $12 15 net value in favor of each head of stock owned in Oregon that year, over and above the net value of each head owned in Maine.

The difference would be greater even than this if the expense and labor of housing, and feeding out the hay were taken into account; and when it is remembered that hay does not constitute the entire feed of stock in cold climates, but that grain, straw, rutabagas, etc., form an important item, the disadvantage under which Maine labors appears still worse. The discrepancy is not so great in the case of some of the States of the Mississippi

Valley; but even there, it is an undetermined question whether the cost of raising stock does not exceed its value when ready for market.

The following are the prices of live stock in the Willamette Valley April 1st, 1870, as near as can be ascertained : Saddle horses, $80 to $100; ordinary work horses suitable for farm work, $100 to $125: stage horses, $100 to $150; draught horses, $150 to $200; good carriage horses $200; team mules, $250 to $350 a pair; work cattle per yoke, (an average) $100; milch, cows, $40 to $50 for good ones; two year old heifers, $20 to $30; yearlings $12 to $15; sheep, $1 50 to $2 50; Beef cattle, per pound, net, 6½ to 7 cts.; fat hogs, 7 cts.; Mutton sheep, $2 50 to $3 50 a piece.

In other parts of the State prices do not vary materially from the above, except that in and around the mining camps they are a little higher.

To give an idea of what is now being done in this branch of industry we append an extract from an article on the "Resources of Oregon," written by the present Editor of the Portland *Evening Commercial*, a gentleman thoroughly informed on the subject of which he writes :

"Much attention is given to the breeding of thoroughbred and good blood stock in Oregon—horses, cattle, sheep, and hogs, and in the Eastern division of the State, to the breeding of fine mules also. Noted sires and dams have been brought from Kentucky and other States to improve the already good native stock of horses, and from these have sprung splendid racers, fast trotters and roadsters, and carriage and draft and work horses of such quality as to command the highest prices in the horse markets of California and Nevada. Durham and other famous breeds of cattle have been brought from Illinois, New York and New Jersey ; also the best breeds of Spanish and French Merinos, Cotswolds, Southdown, and other celebrated or favorite sheep, from Vermont, New York, England and Australia, for wool and mutton both ; and White Cheshire, Essex and Berkshire hogs, are to be found throughout the State, imported direct from England or the East."

Rate of Wages at Portland---in Gold Coin.

Bakers, per mo. and bd...	$40 00 to	60 00	Clerks, pr mo	$50 00 to	75 00
Bar Tenders, per mo	60 00 to	100 00	Coachmen, per mo. & bd.	30 00 to	40 00
Barbers "	60 00 to	90 00	Confectioners, " "		60 00
Blacksmiths. per day	3 50 to	5 00	Cooks, " "	30 00 to	75 00
Blacksmith's helpers,	2 00 to	2 75	Coopers, piece work, for		
Boiler Makers, per day	3 50 to	5 00	Pork barrels	87c.	
Book Binders, per week..		25 00	Fish "	75c.	
Book Keepers, per mo	75 00 to	100 00	Butter Kegs	50c.	
Boot Makers, piece	4 50 to	7 00	Coppersmiths, per day...	5 00 to	6 00
Bricklayers, per day	5 00 to	6 00	Curriers & Tanners, per		
Brick Makers per mo.&bd	40 00 to	60 00	month & board	65 00 to	85 00
Brick Moulders, "	70 00 to	80 00	Deckhands, per mo. & bd	40 00 to	50 00
Brewers, "	75 00 to	100 00	Dish Washers, " "	25 00 to	30 00
Broom Makers, per mo	65 00 to	90 00	Door & Sash Makers, per		
Butchers, per mo. and bd		50 00	day	3 50 to	4 00
Cabinet Makers per day...	3 00 to	3 50	Draymen, per day	2 50 to	3 00
Carpenters " "	3 00 to	4 00	Druggists, per month.		75 00
Carriage Makers "	3 50 to	4 00	Engineers, per mo. & bd	70 00 to	100 00
Carriage Painters "	3 50 to	4 00	Farm hands, " "	25 00 to	30 00
Carvers, per day	4 00 to	5 00	Firemen, " " "	50 00 to	60 00

Fishermen, " "	$25 00 to	40 00
Do., experienced " "	50 00 to	80 00
Gardeners, " "	30 00 to	40 00
Gas Fitters, per day......	3 00 to	3 50
Grocers Help, pr mo.&bd	30 00 to	35 00
Grooms, " "	30 00 to	40 00
Harness Makers, per day	3 50 to	4 00
Hod Carriers, "	3 00 to	3 50
Iron Moulders, per day...	3 50 to	4 00
Laborers " ...	1 50 to	2 50
Laborers (on public work) per day.....	2 00 to	2 50
Do., Railroads, pr mo.&bd		30 00
Lumbermen, " "	30 00 to	45 00
" per day.....	2 50 to	3 00
Machinists, "	3 50 to	4 00
Marble Cutters, "	5 00 to	6 00
Masons (stone), "	5 00 to	6 00
Millers, per mo.............	75 00 to	150 00
Millwrights, per day......	4 00 to	5 00
Nurses, per mo. & board	30 00 to	40 00
Ox Teamsters, " "	40 00 to	50 00
Ostlers & Teamsters " "	30 00 to	45 00
Painters (House), per day		4 00
Pattern Makers, "	3 50 to	4 50
Plasterers, "		5 00
Plumbers, "		4 00
Porters, per month.........	60 00 to	75 00
Printers, per.1000 ems.....	50 to	60
" per week.........	20 00 to	25 00

Salesmen, per mo. ....$50 00 to		100 00
Sailors, per mo. & bd.....		30 00
Sawyers, per day...........		4 00
" per mo. & board	80 00 to	90 00
Stewards, " "	40 00 to	50 00
Stone Cutters, per day.....	5 00 to	6 00
Tailors, "	3 50 to	5 00
Teachers(CountrySchools), per month & board......	30 00 to	40 00
Do., large Schools, pr mo	75 00 to	100 00
Tinsmiths, per day.........	3 50 to	4 00
Truck Drivers, per month	75 00 to	85 00
Upholsterers, per day......	3 00 to	4 00
Wagon Makers, "	3 00 to	4 00
Waiters, per mo. & bd.....	25 00 to	30 00
Watchmakers. per day.....	4 00 to	5 00
Watchmen, per month.....	50 00 to	60 00
Wood Choppers, per cord	1 00 to	1 50
FEMALE.		
Gen. Housework, pr mo. and board..................	20 00 to	30 00
Nurses, per month & bd		30 00
Cooks (in fam.), " "		30 00
Chamber Work (hotel), per month & board......		30 00
Milliners, pr mo. &board		50 00
Seamstresses, per day		1 50
Teachers, pe mo............	35 00 to	50 00
Dress Makers, per day...		1 50
Washerwomen, "	2 00 to	2 50

Nearly all kinds of labor finds ready employment as a general thing. There are exceptions, however, in the case of certain kinds of mechanical labor, such as, Coppersmiths, Boiler Makers, Watchmakers, Bookbinders, and some others, for which a new country can offer employment only to a limited extent. Outdoor labor is interrupted more or less during the rainy season, on account of the weather. Good farm hands are always in demand. Carpenters, bricklayers, millwrights and mechanics of that class find steady employment for three fourths of the year; for the remainder, it is more or less uncertain, depending on the weather. The demand for bookkeepers, clerks, salesmen, bartenders and all that class of employments, is limited. Female house help finds constant employment at the figures named, in good families; and the supply is not near equal to the demand.

In a general sense all kinds of manual labor can obtain employment at fair wages, and those who are industrious, prudent and economical, do not often fail to get along well, even though there is some time lost during the rainy season. Good school teachers usually have no difficulty in obtaining situations; still, where the population is scanty, as it is in Oregon, the demand cannot be very great.

The above rate of wages is intended to apply to Portland and vicinity, especially; with some trifling variations, the rates will hold good throughout Western Oregon. In Eastern Oregon some classes of labor rates considerably higher. For example, farm hands, in the neighborhood of the mining camps receive ordinarily from $30 to $40 per month and board; and laborers in the mines, during the mining season command from 3 00 to $5 00 per day.

MINERAL RESOURCES.

The first gold mines were discovered, in Oregon, in 1850, in Jackson and Josephine counties, in the southern part of the State. Some years afterwards quite extensive placers were opened in Douglass county on the tributaries of the Umpqua river. All these yielded immense returns for the first few years, and afforded employment to a considerable proportion of the gold hunting population that found its way to the Pacfic Coast in the early times of California. At the present time these placers, although skimmed over, and stripped by the labors of more than half a genertiaon, of their surface wealth, still form no insignificant part of the natural resources of the State. Fully one fourth of the population of those districts are engaged directly in the occpation of mining, and not less than three fourths are dependent in some way, directly or indirectly, on the annual yield of the placers for their success in business. The yield of gold from the mines of Southern Oregon, for the past ten years cannot fall short of an average of one million per annum. It is a cash market, at home, for the farm and dairy products of almost the entire southern part of western Oregon. A season of uncommon depth of snow in the mountains, and consequently, of high water in all the creeks and streams, during spring and early summer, makes flush times, not only with miners themselves, who rely on the fall of snow or rain to fill their ditches and carry on their washings, but to the farmer, merchant, and mechanic, who supplies the miner with the necessaries of life. Ten years ago, it was said that, these mines were exhausted, but they have yielded ten million dollars since then, and still hundreds of men find profitable employment in working them. New placers are found occasionally; old ones that had been carelessly skimmed in the feverish haste of the early mining days are being re-opened and often made to yield as well as at first, by means of better appliances for saving the gold.

Gold mines were discovered in Grant and Baker counties, in Eastern Oregon, in 1861, and have been worked continuously every year since then. Like the mines of Southern Oregon, they are mostly placers, located on the bars, banks and in the beds of streams, and depend on heavy snows in the mountains and an abundance of water for successful working. They furnish constant employment to something like two thousand men. Like the mines of Southern Oregon, they are said to be worked out; still they ship to San Francisco every year over a million dollars in gold dust.

There can be no doubt that the cream of the placer mines has been taken. Rich strikes, once common in all the mining districts, are now of very rare occurrence. Big fortunes are not made in a day in the mines, any more than they are anywhere else; but still, laboring men find profitable employment in them. Industry and economy are all that are necessary in mining, as well as other avocations, to acquire substantial competence.

Coal mining is carried on at Coos Bay to a considerable extent. The principal vein at that point extends along a ridge bordering the bay, convenient of access for twelve or fifteen miles, and is being worked at present by two companies. The coal is a good quality of soft or bituminous coal, and finds ready sale in San Francisco. Vessels are constantly loading at the mines and departing for that market. The coal deposit has been worked about fifteen years, and promises to be inexhaustible. Coal of the same variety has been found in large quantities at several other points on the coast. At Port Orford and Yaquina Bay attempts on a small scale, have been made at mining and marketing it, generally with indifferent success, for want of sufficient capital. Near St. Helens, on the Columbia River, an extensive bed of coal has been discovered, and a small amount of work done towards opening and developing it. Deposits have also been found in Clackamas, Clatsop and Tillamook counties as well as in the adjoining counties of Washington Territory, all of which promise, from their extent, quality and conveniences for shipping, to afford profitable employment for labor and capital at no distant day.

Extensive beds of iron ore exist at several points in the Northwestern part of the State. At Oswego, six miles above Portland, on the banks of the Willamette river, the Oregon Iron Co. has erected works for reducing the ore of an extensive deposit in that neighborhood. The works of this Company, although of small capacity, have supplied the foundries of the State with pig iron for the past three years and shipped considerable quantities to the San Francisco market besides. The iron is of very fine compact grain, superior for most kinds of work to the best Scotch pig.

Notwithstanding the value to the State of its gold placers, and the attractions they may have formed to previous immigrations, there can be no question now, but that the future mineral wealth of Oregon is in its resources of coal and iron now hidden in the mountain ranges. Taken in connection with the great productiveness of the soil, the great quantity of timber on every hand, and other conditions that adapt the State to general manufacturing purposes, and this vast supply of mineral wealth assumes a peculiar importance. But Oregon has not had time to accumulate the capital necessary for the development of either her mineral or other resources. Situated in a far-off corner of the United States, remote from the centres of population and routes of travel, immigrations hither have generally been prompted by the inducements offered for making permanent homes in the rich valleys for an agricultural people. The people of Oregon came here poor ; a large number of them brought their families from the Mississippi to the Willamette, overland, a distance of 2,500 miles, in ox teams. They have not only made a settlement on the confines of the continent, but have subdued the wild forces of nature and still wilder savages, and laid the foundations of a great State. To develop its natural wealth, time is necessary, and capital and population must be accumulated.

MANUFACTURING INTERESTS.

In the various branches of manufacturing industry Oregon has barely made a commencement, notwithstanding her great capacities in that line. The leading manufacturing establishments now in operation are six woolen mills, located as follows : One at Oregon City, one at Salem, one at Brownsville, one at Dallas, one at Ashland and one at the Dalles ; an oil mill at Salem ; a paper mill at Clackamas, together with quite a large number of flouring mills. The Willamette woolen mills, located at Salem, the oldest and largest of that class of establishments, consumes annually about 400,000 pounds of wool and employs in the neighborhood of one hundred hands regularly. The blankets, flannels, cassimeres and other goods made by this and similar establishments in the State have been put on exhibition in Eastern cities repeatedly, always eliciting the highest praise, and frequently taking premiums at the industrial fairs of other States. The cost of manufacturing these goods is low enough to cause them to enter very largely into general use, not only in Oregon, but in Idaho, Montana and Washington Territories, excluding to a great extent imported goods from these markets.

The Pioneer Oil Mill, at Salem, manufactured 60,000 gallons of linseed oil last year, and expects to turn out 100,000 gallons in 1870. It is in contemplation to establish a linen factory in connection with the oil mill, as farmers are turning their attention to flax growing. It may reasonably be expected that this branch of manufacturing industry will become an important one in a few years.

The Clackamas Paper Mills are confined to the manufacture of straw, manilla, hardware and news paper. The mills have a capacity of two thousand pounds per diem with twenty-five hands. The ordinary running force is from twelve to fourteen hands, producing one thousand pounds a day, of an excellent quality, which finds ready sale in a home market.

Among the large flouring mills of the State may be enumerated the Standard Mills, at Milwaukie, the Imperial Mills, at Oregon City; the Salem Mills, at Salem, and the Magnolia Mills at Albany. These have a capacity of from 300 to 500 barrels of flour every twenty four hours. A great many others scattered throughout the farming districts of the state, of smaller capacity supply the necessary facilities for converting into flour, and marketing the wheat crops of their respective neighborhoods. The estimation in which Oregon flour is held in San Francisco, may be inferred from the following extract taken from a late number of the *Commercial Herald* of that city.

"The arrivals of Flour and Wheat from Oregon continue liberal, as will be found elsewhere detailed. The better brands of Extra which reach us from our sister State, enter largely into the local trade of the city. Many of our bakers, hotels and large consumers giving it a preference over all others, simply by reason of its strength, having more gluten, and therefore requiring more water in its preparation, making a larger loaf, and consequently esteemed more profitable."

Among the minor but equally important branches of mechanical and manufacturing industry, are sash, door and other woodworking shops, tanneries, distilleries, carding machines, foundries and machine shops; all of these calculated merely, to supply the local demands. The iron foundries and machine shops of Portland have excellent facilities for supplying the wants of the country with all articles in that line, but nothing is manufactured for export.

The resources of the state in timber, iron ore and coal together with the wonderful fertility of its soil and the great amount of water power, should make Oregon a great manufacturing State. The climate is adapted to wool growing to a degree equal if not superior to that of any other State, yet fully one half the

wool crop goes to San Francisco to market every year, notwithstanding the manufacture of woolen goods has received more
attention from the people than any other class of manufactures.
The few small tanneries at work in different parts of the state
do not near supply the country with leather. Large numbers
of hides are shipped to San Francisco annually and leather for
the ordinary wants of the people imported, which by the introduction of labor and capital could be made at home; for the
hemlock and other bark produced in enormous quantities in the
Oregon mountains, has no superior for tanning purposes. Almost all the agricultural implements in use are imported from
New York, yet all the raw material is here in great abundance
for their manufacture.

The growth of the country and the expansion of the agricultural interest from year to year, increases the demand for nearly all manufactured articles; but like all new countries in this
respect, manufacturers are of slow growth, and must wait for
the necessary capital to be accumulated or the introduction of
it from other quarters.

LUMBERING RESOURCES.

It has already been stated that the mountain ranges of Oregon are heavily timbered. But that term, in the sense in which
it would be used in nearly all the Eastern States, conveys no
adequate idea of the immense forests which clothe the Cascade
and Coast ranges of mountains. The principal lumbering establishments are located on the Columbia river below the junction
of the Willamette, and at various points on the coast, where inlets, bays and arms of the sea, provide safe anchorage for small
craft, and where the forests are easy of access from navigable
water. In the interior of the State are many small mills erected
for the purpose of supplying their own immediate neighborhoods,
conducted solely with reference to that object.

The varieties of timber adapted to general lumbering purposes, are, the red, white and yellow fir, cedar, spruce, hemlock,
and in some parts of the interior pine and larch. The yellow
fir is the main dependence for all purposes requiring strength
and elasticity. It enters into general use for building, fencing,
bridges, wharves, piles, spars, and ship timber. Cedar is used
for finishing material, for posts, and in foundations where it will
come in contact with the ground, on account of its durable qual-
ities in such situations. An excellent quality of ash is obtained

along the streams and on the low lands in western Oregon, suitable for many different mechanical purposes; but there is no hickory or other timber suitable for wagon and carriage work. All that kind of timber used is imported from the Atlantic seaboard, although oak of a fair quality can be procured in places. Maple and alder are abundant and of good quality for cabinet work, for which they are used almost exclusively.

Lumber, like other Oregon products, finds its principal market at San Francisco, and in the southern part of California. The agricultural portions of that State are destitute of timber. The cities and coast valleys particularly, rely entirely on the saw mills of Oregon and Washington Territory for building, fencing, wharf, bridge and ship timber. In addition to San Francisco, a large market for Oregon lumber exists at the sea-ports of Mexico, South America, Sandwich Islands, China, Japan and Australia. Cargoes of lumber have been shipped from the Columbia River to New York and Liverpool with profit. Considering the rapidly increasing demand for lumber and timber of all descriptions, at all these places, it is safe to presume that the market for Oregon lumber will continue to be good; and considering the approaching scarcity of the article in what has been hitherto considered good timber countries, the great supply in the forests of Oregon and Washington Territory, together with the natural advantages for marketing commanded by lumbermen there, will put all thought of serious or dangerous competition out of the way.

Extensive lumbering establishments are now in operation at the following places on the the coast of Oregon, commencing at the southern boundary of the State and going north : Ellensburg, at the mouth of Rogue River, Port Orford, Randolph, at the mouth of the Coquille, Coos Bay, the mouth of the Umpqua and Yaquina Bay. Coos Bay is the principal one of these points, partly on account of its lumber trade, and partly on account of its coal. The two together have been the means of building up quite a considerable commerce although the population is small. There are three large mills in operation there, having a joint capacity of 75,000 feet of miscellaneous lumber every ten hours, when in ordinary running order. They are all driven by steam. The mill owners have their own vessels, especially constructed for the purpose of transporting their lumber to market. About 20,000,000 feet is shipped from this place every year. Notwithstanding the drain upon the timber on the shores of the bay, carried on at this rate for the past ten or a dozen years, the supply is still large enough to offer inducements for the erection of other mills of larger capacity and power than any of those now at work. At Portland there are three mills in operation having a joint capacity of 45,000 feet in ten hours. Their business is confined to the manufacture of lumber for the local market. The machinery consists of the ordinary double circular, edgers, trimmers, lath saws, slab saws and the necessary planing and other dressing machinery to meet the wants of the market for dressed lumber, all driven by stean power. Their logs cost $5, coin, per M, delivered in the boom at the mills. Labor costs them, in gold, $4 per day for head sawyer, $5 for hands with the planing and dressing machinery, and from $2 to $3 for all other classes of labor. They receive for lumber the following rates, (April 1st 1870): Street lumber, $11, to $12; miscellaneous rough lumber, $14, to $15; flooring, $26 to $28; siding, $20 to $21; miscellaneous lumber, dressed, from $20 to $31,—all in gold. These rates include the delivery of the lumber to any part of the city. The three mills turned out the past year about 7,600,000 feet of lumber of all grades, all of which was consumed in the city.

On the Columbia river below the junction of the Willamette, there are a number of small mills in operation. Two of the largest have a capacity of 15,000 feet per day, each. The others average from 3,000 to 10,000 feet per day. One is now in course of construction at the mouth of the river, calculated to cut from 40,000 to 50,000 feet every ten hours. A small part of the lumber made on the lower Columbia is consumed at Portland; the bulk of it goes to San Francisco, China, South America, the Sandwich Islands and Mexico. The expenses of running a sawmill on the Columbia, are a little less than at Portland. Logs cost less by a dollar or dollar and a half per M., and the cost of labor is somewhat less, particularly, unskilled labor. The mills are generally located on the bank of the river or a navigable slough or tributary, for the convenience of shipping the lumber, as well as for getting logs to the mills economically. The price of lumber at these mills is always determined by the San Francisco price, that being the principal market. Freight to San Franciso by sailing vessels, is now $6 per M.; the San Francisco price for miscellaneous rough lumber is $16, leaving the lumberman $10 as the net price of his lumber at the mill. Lumber, like all other commodities, fluctuates more or less at the leading markets; the prices are now "down." From $20 to $22 is about the highest range in San Francisco for common lumber when the market is active and prices up.

Some business is done on the Columbia in ship timber, spars and piles. China is the chief market for light spars and San Francisco for piles and heavy timber. There is little or nothing done in heavy spars, or masts, as Puget Sound supples the markets with them. The saw mills of the Columbia, like those of other places in Oregon and Washington Territory, use the double circular, and the usual edging, trimming and dressing machinery, driven in some cases by water, and in others by steam power. Taken in the aggregate, they manufacture and send to market every year, a large quantity of lumber of every grade; but no single establishment is wielded with sufficient capital to make its business so enormously large as in the case of the Port Gamble, Port Orchard and other establishments on Puget Sound. But this circumstance is not owing to a lack of natural facilities, or, of the raw material; for the sloping hill sides, descending to the banks of the river on both sides, from the Willamette to the sea, a distance of a hundred miles, are clothed with a dense compact growth to the water's edge, of all the varieties of timber common to the Northwest coast. Experienced lumbermen estimate that the timber within one mile of the navigable waters of the Columbia, suitable for saw logs, cannot be exhausted by the saw mill force now in operation, during the present generation. Many times, a hundred thousand feet of lumber have been taken from an acre of ground and it is not uncommon for six to eight thousand feet to be obtained from a single tree. The usual rate of stumpage is 50 cts. per M. when logs are obtained in that way. Generally, mill owners buy the lands and have the logs delivered by contract. The method adopted for getting the logs to the mills is, to haul them to the water's edge on wheels, from the place of cutting, generally not over a few hundred yards, then, after getting them into the water, they are made into rafts, to be floated to the mill, if down stream, or towed by a small tug, if they are to go up stream. Timbered lands well situated for logging purposes are held at from $8 to $15 per acre. Within three miles of the river, government lands can be obtained in any quantity.

FISHERIES.

The salmon is the principal fish of Oregon waters. It is noted among the most delicious of its species in any part of the world; and is so plentiful in its season, that it has constituted the principal article of food for the Indian tribes of the country from time immemorial. It enters largely into general consumption as an article of diet, with the present population, during the spring and summer. The salmon fisheries of the Columbia river have become an important branch of Oregon industry. Until within the last few years they were worked almost exclusively by Indians and half breeds, producing a few barrels of fish annually to be exchanged for a few necessary supplies. Now they engage the attention of capital amounting to many thousands of dollars, and the labor of several hundred men.

The heaviest business is done by the canning establishments, of which there are four, employing in the aggregate about two hundred men during the busy season, and from eight to ten each, the remainder of the year. The process of canning salmon has been lately introduced. It consists in cooking and seasoning the fish ready for the table, after which it is put, while hot, into tin cans, containing each one and two pounds, and hermetically sealed. The cans are then packed in cases of two dozen two-pound, or four dozen one-pound cans, in a case, for shipment. There is but little local demand for the article thus prepared, on account of the large supply and low price of fresh salmon. But it has been introduced into foreign markets with great success.

Export statistics show that San Francisco received from the Columbia river during the year 1869, 22,130 cases of canned salmon. Two dozen cans to the case would amount to 531,120 cans, shipped to San Francisco alone. A considerable portion of this, however, was forwarded to New York city. The estimate of some persons intimately acquainted with the business is that the product of canned salmon for the year 1869, would reach an aggregate of 800,000 cans.

The canning houses are provided with the necessary boats, nets and other appliances for catching the fish, and generally rely on their own catch to supply the cannery, although the practice is coming into vogue of buying fish from others who carry on fishing on a small scale, without sufficient capital to conduct the canning business. The price paid in such cases, ranges from 20 to 30 cents a piece. The average weight of the

Columbia river salmon is from 20 to 25 pounds. The cost of labor connected with the catching and canning business is, from $50 to 80 per month and board, for experienced hands; $25 to 40 for ordinary hands, and from $15 to 20 for boys and young men to work about the canneries.

The class of nets used are what are technically called "Gill nets." They are "floated" or "drifted" and the fish hauled into the boats. A net of 100 fathoms length and 20 feet depth costs in the neighborhood of $140, and boats cost from $100 to 125. Each cannery has its own machinery for the manufacture of cans, the material for which is purchased in large quantities and at wholesale prices.

Aside from the canneries, about one hundred men are engaged in Salmon fishing, generally in parties, of from two to six, who have their own nets, boats and tackle, and carry oh business, either to supply the Portland market with fresh fish, or salt and can their fish, to be marketed in Portland, whence it is shipped to San Francisco or to the Sandwich Islands. The different methods of curing are, first, by salting down in barrels; salting and smoking; and salting and pickling in small kits for family use. The consumption in Portland and the interior towns, of fish cured in all these different ways, is quite considerable. During the year 1869, the shipments of salted salmon to San Francisco amounted to 3,792 barrels and 4,746 half barrels. The amount of capital required to carry on the business of catching and salting is not so large but that it can be prosecuted by men of moderate means. Fish barrels cost $1 75 a piece; half barrels $1 25; Salt of the kind used in the business costs $25 per ton at Portland. The usual price of salted salmon at Portland is from $9 to 10 per barrel.

The fishing season commences about the first of April and lasts until the last of July. There is usually a full run of salmon, but the fish are not as good as the spring run.

Sturgeon, tom-cod, flounder and smelt are very plentiful in the Columbia; and mountain and brook trout, in all the small streams throughout the country. The market is plentifully supplied with all these in the season.

Oyster fishing is carried on to some extent at Shoalwater Bay in Washington Territory and at Yaquina Bay in Oregon. At the first named place about 100 men are emplyed one way and another. At Yaquina Bay, the number is not so large, nor the facilities for culture as good. The oysters of both places are small but of fine flavor. They find a ready market at Portland and in the interior towns of Oregon and at San Francisco.

SCHOOLS.

The school fund of this State is under the management of a Board of Commissioners, consisting of the Governor, Secretary of State and State Treasurer, who loan the fund at the rate of 10 per cent. per annum interest, secured by mortgage on real estate. This fund amounted in 1868 to $242,228, bringing an annual interest of $24,222, to be distributed by law to the several counties for common school purposes; the amount to which each county is entitled, being determined by a census of its children of the lawful age to entitle them to the benefit of the fund.

Each county levies a tax yearly, for common school purposes; and each school district is authorized by law to levy a tax, in addition, sufficient to make the schools free to all, and to keep them open the entire year; this is the case in all the larger towns and most populous districts. For example:

The school fund of Linn county, this year, is $5,597, to be divided among 4,245 scholars, giving $1 32 to each scholar; in Lane county, the fund is $3,262, to be divided among 2,773 scholars, giving to each $1 18; in Polk county the fund is $3,037, No. of scholars 2,144, amount per scholar $1 42; in Marion county, amount of fund $6,300, No. of scholars 4,457, amount per scholar $1 39½. These respective amounts are exclusive of the tax, levied in the several districts by the voters thereof, which may be made sufficient to keep open the schools the entire year. or not, at their option.

To illustrate this point: School District No. 1 of Multnomah county, which embraces the City of Portland, contains according to a census of February 1870, 2,117 scholars. The apportionment of the State and county school fund to the district was $7,446 75. The amount of taxable property in the district is $5,303,511 on which was levied at a meeting of voters a tax of 2½ mills on the dollar, aggregating $13,258 78. Of this $11,830 was collected which together with the State and county fund, the balance on hand from the year previous and some collections of deliquent taxes, made an aggregate of $23,332. The disbursements amounted to $17,752, leaving $5,581 in the Treasury. The disbursements include $12,417 for pay of teachers.

The District owns six school houses and the grounds occupied by them. Three quarters, of fourteen weeks each, were taught in all the schools.

The land in the State for school purposes is—
1st—The 16th and 36th sections in each township of the public lands;
2d—Seventy-two sections for the State University;
3d—Five hundred thousand acres granted by Congress, Sept. 4th, 1841;
4th—Ninety thousand acres for an Agricultural College.

The University fund has about ten thousand dollars on hand With a quarter of a million dollars on hand and the receipts from the sale of school lands, Oregon has in the near future a magnificient endowment for her common schools; ample to afford a good English education; free, to every child in the State. The people have always devoted great attention to the question of education, and there can be no danger that they will ever permit the diversion of this fund from its legitimate purpose under any pretense whatever.

The higher schools supported by tuition and endowments are:

One in Jackson county,	Catholic.	One in Marion county,	Catholic.
One in Douglas "	Methodist.	One in Polk "	Methodist.
One in Benton "	Presbyterian.	One in Polk "	Independent.
One in Benton "	Episcopal.	One in Yamhill "	Baptist.
One in Benton "	S. Methodist.	One in Washington "	Congregational.
One in Linn "	Presbyterian.	Two in Multnomah "	Episcopal.
One in Linn "	Methodist.	One in Multnomah "	Catholic.
Two in Marion "	"	One in Multnomah ".	Methodist.

These are all good schools, conducted under the auspices of the several denominations of the Christian church, and, except the Catholic, can hardly be deemed sectarian.

The Willamette University at Salem, and the Pacific University at Forest Grove, have fine buildings and about fifty thousand dollars endowment, each..

For its population, there is no State in the Union more liberally provided with educational facilities.

GENERAL LAWS.

PROPERTY RIGHTS OF MARRIED WOMEN.—The constitution of Oregon provides:

"That the property and pecuniary rights of every married women at the time of her marriage, or afterwards acquired by gift, devise or inheritance, shall not be subject to the debts or contracts of the husband; and laws shall be passed providing for the registration of the wife's separate property"

SPECIFIC PERFORMANCE OF COIN CONTRACTS.—A statute of Oct. 1864, provides:

"That the several courts in giving judgment or decree on a written contract for the payment or delivery of gold coin, &c., shall, if either party require it, adjudge or decree, that the principal sum and interest so contracted to be paid or delivered, shall be paid in the kind of money specified in such contract."

Under this law gold or coin contracts are specifically enforced and transactions by *written* contract to pay coin are more numerous than contracts for currency. The custom of the country is to transact all business on a gold basis, and when *legal tenders* are used, they are taken at their value in gold, determined by the New York or San Francisco quotations. State and county taxes are payable in coin.

INTEREST ON MONEY.—The legal rate when there is a contract to pay interest and no rate specified, is ten per cent. per annum. But by express agreement of parties one per cent. per month may be charged and no more. Violations of this law subject the usurer to the liability of having the entire debt forfeited to the school fund; the debtor, however, is not exonerated from liability to pay, his condition only, is changed.

EXTRACTS FROM THE CONSTITUTION.—The Constitution of the State prohibits the Legislature from

Incorporating any bank or other monied institution, or from authorizing any bank to issue bills or checks, or other paper to circulate as money.

Corporations may be formed under general laws, but shall not be created by special laws, except for municipal purposes Stockholders in all corporations and joint stock companies shall be liable for the debts of their respective companies to the amount of their stock subscribed and unpaid, and no more.

Acts of the legislative Assembly incorporating towns and cities shall restrict their powers of taxation, borrowing money, contracting debts and loaning their credit.

The State shall not subscribe to, or be interested in the stock of any corporation, company or association.

No county, city or other municipal corporation by vote of its citizens or otherwise, shall become a stockholder in any joint stock company, corporation or association, whatever, or loan its credit to, or in aid of any such company or association.

The legislative Assembly shall not loan the credit of the State, or create any debts or liabilities, which singly or in the aggregate with previous debts or liabilities shall exceed the sum of fifty thousand dollars, except in case of war or to repel invasion or suppress insurrection.

The State of Oregon, owing to the wise provisions of its constitution, has comparatively no debt. With the exception of two or three new mining counties, there is no county in the State that has any debt of any consequence. No onerous burdens are imposed upon the people in the form of taxes every year, to pay interest on accumulated debts either State, county or municipal. The rates of taxation in the different counties, for state, county, school and all purposes ranges from fifteen to twenty mills on the dollar, rarely going as high the latter figure.

The laws of the State exempt from sale under execution, in case of distress for debt: the wearing apparel of a family; the tools, teams or vehicles, implements or library, necessary to enable any person to carry on the trade or profession by which he gains a livelihood to the value of four hundred dollars; provisions actually provided for family use and necessary for its support for six months; household goods, furniture and utensils to the value of three hundred dollars, together with two cows, five swine and ten sheep with one year's fleece or the yarn or cloth made therefrom; books, pictures and musical instruments to the value of seventy-five dollars; and the pew, occupied by a householder or family in any place of public worship.

EMIGRANT ROUTES AND COST OF TRAVEL TO OREGON.

From all parts of the country on the Atlantic sea-board there are two practicable routes of travel to Oregon.

1st—By railway across the continent. This is much the most expeditious route of the two, and for emigrants from any point in the Western States is perferable to the other. Through-tickets to San Francisco, can be purchased at all the large cities of the Atlantic States, making the connection with the main line of road at Chicago or Omaha. The usual time consumed in making the trip to San Francisco is about seven days from New York and six days from Chicago. From San Francisco to Portland, Oregon, the trip is made by ocean steamer in about four days, distance 640 miles.

Through Fares to San Francisco, payable in "CURRENCY".

From			1st class cars.	2d class cars.
New York to San Francisco			$140 00	$110 00
Philadelphia "	"		138 00	110 00
Baltimore "	"		137 25	108 75
Chicago "	"		118 00	93 00
St. Louis "	"		118 00	93 00
Omaha "	"		100 00	80 00

Second class cars go with the "Express-Trains".

Children not over 12 years of age, half fare; under five years of age, free.
100 ℔s of baggage to each adult passenger, free.
50 " " " " child between 5 and 12 years, free.
Extra baggage (over 100 ℔s) from Chicago to San Francisco per ℔ 17c.
from Omaha, " " " 15c.
First class freight from Chicago " " " 7½c.
Sleeping accomodations and meals are charged extra. Sleeping berths accomodating two persons cost $22 00 from New York. $17 00 from Chicago and $14 00 from Omaha. Emigrants are allowed to carry provisions with them in the cars, and thereby save considerable expenses in that line.

From San Francisco to Portland by steamer, fare, payable in COIN.

Cabin $36 00; Steerage $20 50; "actual emigrants" in the steerage $12 00; usual allowance of baggage and reductions in favor of the children under 12 years of age. In order that emigrants may avail themselves of the benefits of the "emigrant" rate of fare on the steamer, they must be provided with a certificate to the effect that they are "actual emigrants," from the Board of Immigration at Portland, Oregon, which can be obtained of the Secretary of the Board, by applying by letter; or the certificate can be obtained at the office of the California Emigrant Union, 315 California Street, San Francisco, by furnishing satisfactory evidence that they are actual emi-

grants. Applications by letter should give the name distinctly, and the number of children in each family.

Oregon has connection with the Pacific railroad at two points. Kelton in Utah, and Sacramento, Calitornia. A daily line of stages runs from Kelton through south-western Idaho and north-eastern Oregon to Umatilla on the Columbia river; distance 515 miles; through fare $60 00 COIN : time four days ; 50 lbs of baggage, free. To persons bound for points in Eastern Oregon, or Washington Territory, this is a good route, saving distance and time, but scarcely practicable for families on account of the length of stage travel. The cost this way is about the same as that around by the way of San Francisco and Portland.

From Sacramento a line of railway is in operation, northwardly to Oroville, connecting there with a daily line of stages to Portland; distance 576 miles; through fare from Sacramento to Portland $45 00 COIN; time, six days in summer, twelve days in winter. This route offers inducements to people going into southern Oregon, as the stages cross the entire state from south to north. Fare by this route from Sacramento to Rogue river Valley $40 00; to the Umpqua Valley $45 00—all in coin ; length of stage ride from Oroville to Rogue river Valley, 280 miles; to Umpqua Valley 375 miles; time to each place, three and four days, respectively.

The second main route of travel from the Atlantic sea-board is from New York to San Francisco by ocean steamer, via Panama. The steamers of the Pacific Mail Steamship Company leave New York on the 5th and 21st of each month ; time to San Francisco, 22 days. The fare by this route is somewhat subject to fluctuation, but always lower than the fare by railway. $125 00 in the cabin and $65 00 in the steerage (both in currency) is about the rate. Passengers by this route are allowed a larger quantity of baggage, free, than by railway, and would not have to pay as high rates on extra baggage.

Cost of Travel from Europe.—Payable in gold.

The Liverpool and Great Western Steamship Company sells through thickets to San Francisco, from the several European sea-port towns, at rates as follows :

To San Francisco from	Cabin.	Steerage.
Liverpool and Queenstown	$210 00	$84 00
Hamburg, Amsterdam, Rotterdam, Harlingen and Antwerp	224 00	90 00
Copenhagen, Gothenburg, Christiania, Bergen, Havre, Paris, Manheim	230 00	94 00

Children under 12 half price ; under 1 year $3 50.

Passengers are forwarded from New York by the boats of the Pacific Mail Steamship Company, via Panama. Steamers leave

Liverpool and Queenstown once a week. Steerage passengers are supplied on the ocean passage with medical attendance and good substantial food, free of cost. Owing to the fluctuations in gold in New York, the cost of forwarding passengers from that point to San Francisco is not always the same, hence the through rates from Europe are liable to some variation, though not more than a few dollars, and in any case, emigrants from Europe will find this much the cheaper route.

In case emigrants from Europe should prefer to cross the American continent by rail, the following rates of fare to the United States by the several steamship lines will enable them to estimate the cost; railroad fare from New York and other cities heretofore given.

By the North German Lloyd Steamship line (payable in gold).

		Adult.	Children 1 to 10.	Children under 1 year.
From Bremen, Southampton & Havre				
to Baltimore.....................................Cabin		$100 00	$50 00	$2 00
" " .... Steerage		40 00	20 00	2 00

By the "Anchor Line" of steamers from Glasgow to New York. (STEERAGE: payable in gold).

To New York.

From Glasgow, Londonderry, Liverpool & Queenstown.............................$34 00
Children from 1 to 12 years, half fare.
"   under 1 year, $5 00.
" Hamburg, Antwerp, Rotterdam or Havre 40 00
" Denmark, Norway, Sweden or Paris...... .... 45 00
" Drontheim, Malmo or Stavanger, $3 00 extra.
Children, 1 to 12 years, half fare.
"   under 1 year, free.

From the foregoing tables and descriptions of the different routes any one can easily calculate for himself the cost of travel to Oregon from any point in Europe or United States.

☞ It is reported that a change reducing overland railroad fare will be made after May 1st.

WASHINGTON TERRITORY.

This pamphlet would hardly fulfill the object for which it was written, without, at least, a short description of Washington Territory. The Territory was originally a part of Oregon, from which it was separated by act of Congress, of March 2d 1853, providing its people with a territorial government. It has an area of about 70,000 square miles, and a population of about 40,000. The seat of government is at Olympia, at the the head of Puget Sound. The Territory is divided into eastern and western divisions by the Cascade Mountains, the same as Oregon. It has for its boundaries, British Columbia on the north, Idaho Territory on the east, Oregon on the south, from which it is separated by the Columbia river, and the ocean on the west. It has the same peculiarities of climate, in its eastern and western divisions, that have been described as belonging to Oregon. Lying on the north, it is a trifle colder in winter, and only a trifle, unless, it may be, in the extreme northren part, where the country is mountainous and subject to deep snows, the thermometer in winter indicates a colder climate. The description given of the soil and products of Oregon, will apply equally well to Washington Territory, except that the proportion of good land in the western part, is not so large as in western Oregon. There is less prairie land of good quality, but the timber and brushy lands of the creek and river bottoms are good as can be found anywhere. The principal settlements of the western part are located around Puget sound and on the Columbia river. Although farming is carried on to a considerable extent on the sound, still the leading branch of business there, is the lumber trade. Coal mining and the fisheries are quite important branches of business. The Sound country is good for stock raising, the climate being so mild that but little feeding in winter is required.

Puget Sound is a large inland sea having a length of about 160 miles, with an entrance from the sea in the northwestern corner of the territory. With its numerous inlets, channels and bays, it affords shipping facilities rarely met with in any part of the world.

The eastern part of Washington Territory has the same characteristics of soil and products as eastern Oregon. The principal settlements are in the south east corner, in the Walla Walla and other valleys. Walla Walla county, embracing nearly all these valleys, has an area of about 3,500,000 acres; 418,-000 acres arable land; the remainder pasture and timber. About 165,000 acres have been entered under the pre-emption and homestead laws and by cash purchase. The population of the county is about 7,000 souls, the taxable property amounting to $1,822,-752. The average yield of farm products per acre is: 25 bushels of wheat; 30 of oats; 30 of barley; 40 of corn; 20 of rye; 40 of peas; 500 of potatoes: 300 of sweet potatoes and 1000 of carrots. Fruit of all kinds succeeds well. The county is bounded on two sides by the navigable waters of the Columbia and Snake rivers, but the principal markets are in the mining regions of the adjacent territories. The prices of farm products, stock and other commodities, as well as the rate of wages, differ but little from those of eastern Oregon.

There is a very large amount of vacant land in both the eastern and western parts of the territory, to be obtained by settlers, under the homestead and pre-emption laws, and in some localities by cash purchase.

The advantages of churches and schools are not as good as in Oregon; the country is more sparsely settled and newer; the people have not had the opportunity to build up institutions of that kind. But in this respect it is improving gradually; the people are generally of a class that appreciate the advantages to society of such institutions, and are making commendable efforts to place their school system on a sound basis, as well as to preserve and regulate the moral tone of society.

About the only general idea that can be given of the price of improved land in Washington Territory, is, that it sells at about what the improvements would cost, except that in a few particular localities it may be a little higher. Settlements in the territory, cluster around a few centers. Near these the land has been taken, good, bad, and indifferent. Outside of these settlements, almost the entire territory is vacant. A good authority estimates the arable land of the western part of the territory at 6,000,000 acres, and while it is true that the prairies are generally taken, it is conceded to be equally true that the best lands, embracing the alder flats on creek bottoms are mostly unoccupied. The Chehalis and Willopah valleys contain upwards of 300,000 acres of vacant land. These valleys produce abundantly all kinds of grain, grass, vegetables and fruits, commonly grown in a temperate climate, except corn, peaches, and a few tender varieties of vegetables. The climate and soil of the territory adapted for the homes of men. It is capable of supporting a vast population, and offers abundant rewards for the industry of the farmer, mechanic, lumberman and other industrial classes.

9 7 8 3 3 3 7 1 4 8 4 4 7